AI Whispers: Decoding the Silent Language of Machines

Vishakha Marwah

Front cover design by ***Dalveer Singh Marwah***

This work is guarded by ***Dalsi Music Studio company.***

First Digital Edition: ***February 18, 2025***

This is the first digital edition of this work. It is made available exclusively.

Made with ♥ on the ***Notion Press Platform***

www.notionpress.com

Dedication

To my pillars of strength and inspiration,
Smt. Asha Jangde and Shri Jagannath Jangde

With profound gratitude and admiration, I dedicate this work to my parents, whose unwavering support and countless sacrifices have been the foundation of my journey. Your resilience in the face of hardships, your tireless efforts to provide for our family, and your enduring belief in the power of education have shaped not only my life but the very essence of this book.

Mother, your quiet strength and endless patience have taught me perseverance.
Father, your wisdom and principled approach to life have instilled in me the values that guide my path.

The pages that follow are a testament to the love, dedication, and selflessness you have shown throughout your lives. Your story of overcoming challenges to raise our family with dignity and hope continues to inspire me every day.

This book stands as a humble tribute to your lifelong commitment to our family's growth and well-being. May it serve as a small token of my eternal gratitude for the immeasurable gifts you have given me.

With love and respect,

Vishakha

Decoding AI: Your Path Through the Book

Preface

In the ever-evolving landscape of technology, artificial intelligence stands as a beacon of innovation, promise, and, for some, trepidation. As we find ourselves on the cusp of a new era where machines not only compute but also 'think', 'decide', and 'communicate', it becomes imperative to decode the silent language that underpins these artificial minds.

"AI Whispers: Decoding the Silent Language of Machines" is born out of a fascination with the intricate dance between human ingenuity and machine capability. This book aims to demystify the complex world of AI communication, offering readers a unique glimpse into the 'conversations' happening within and between artificial intelligence systems.

As an author deeply immersed in the field of AI, I've often found myself marveling at the subtle yet profound ways in which these systems interact—with data, with each other, and with us. This book is my attempt to share that wonder, to bridge the gap between technical jargon and everyday understanding, and to explore the implications of this silent language on our future.

Within these pages, you'll embark on a journey from the birth of machine language to the ethical considerations of AI decision-making. We'll explore pattern recognition, decision trees, and the future of human-AI collaboration. My hope is that by the end of this book, you'll not only have a clearer understanding of how AI 'thinks' and 'communicates' but also a newfound appreciation for the potential and challenges that lie ahead.

It's worth noting that this book itself is a testament to the collaborative potential between human creativity and AI assistance. In crafting this work, I've embraced AI tools as a partner in the writing process, allowing for a unique blend of human insight and machine-aided efficiency. This approach has enabled me to bring this book to life in a remarkably short time frame, without compromising on depth or quality.

As we stand at the threshold of an AI-augmented future, it's crucial that we, as a society, engage in informed discussions about the role of artificial intelligence in our lives. My sincere hope is that this book will serve as a catalyst for such conversations, inspiring readers to look beyond the surface and listen closely to the whispers of our artificial counterparts.

Welcome to the hidden world of AI communication. Let's decode it together.

Vishakha Marwah

Acknowledgments

No book is ever truly the work of a single individual, and this one is no exception. I owe a debt of gratitude to several people who have supported and inspired me throughout this journey.

First and foremost, I extend my deepest appreciation to my daughter, Preesha. As a bright and inquisitive student at John Monash Science School in Melbourne, your passion for science has been a constant source of inspiration for me. Your insightful questions and enthusiasm for learning have challenged me to explore the complexities of AI in new and meaningful ways.

To my beloved mother, Asha Jangde, and my father, Jagannath Jangde, thank you for your unwavering love, support, and encouragement throughout my life. Your sacrifices and belief in me have made all of this possible.

I would also like to express my sincere gratitude to my teachers, friends, and family. Your collective wisdom, guidance, and unwavering belief in my abilities have been invaluable. Thank you for always being there to lend an ear, offer advice, and provide the encouragement I needed to keep going.

Finally, I extend my appreciation to anyone and everyone who contributed to this work. Your collective efforts have helped bring this book to fruition.

Introduction: The Invisible Conversation

In the bustling digital landscape of 2025, artificial intelligence has become an integral part of our daily lives. From the moment we wake up to our smart home assistants, to the personalized content we consume, to the autonomous vehicles that navigate our streets, AI is constantly at work, silently processing, deciding, and communicating in ways that are often invisible to us.

Yet, for all its ubiquity, the inner workings of AI remain a mystery to many. How do these intelligent systems actually "think"? What language do they speak? And how do they communicate with each other and with us?

"***AI Whispers: Decoding the Silent Language of Machines***" aims to pull back the curtain on this hidden world of artificial intelligence. In this book, we embark on a journey to explore the subtle, complex, and fascinating ways in which AI systems process information, make decisions, and interact with their environment and with humans.

Our exploration will take us through several key areas:

1. The evolution of machine language and how it differs from human communication

2. The intricate patterns that AI systems recognize and interpret in data

3. The fascinating realm of AI-to-AI communication

4. The decision-making processes of AI, including the use of decision trees

5. The ethical implications of AI's silent conversations

6. The future of human-AI interaction and collaboration

As we delve into these topics, we'll uncover the hidden language of machines - a language of algorithms, data structures, and statistical models. We'll see how this language allows AI to perform tasks that once seemed the exclusive domain of human intelligence, from recognizing speech to predicting trends to creating art.

But this book is more than just a technical exploration. It's an invitation to consider the profound implications of AI's silent conversations. How do these invisible exchanges shape our world? What are the ethical considerations we must grapple with as AI becomes more sophisticated and autonomous? And how can we, as humans, best prepare ourselves to collaborate with these artificial intelligences?

As we stand on the cusp of a new era of human-AI collaboration, understanding the language of machines is no longer just the domain of computer scientists and engineers. It's crucial knowledge for anyone who wants to navigate and thrive in our AI-augmented world.

So, let's tune in to the whispers of AI. Let's decode the silent language of machines. And in doing so, let's prepare ourselves for a future where the conversation between humans and artificial intelligence becomes ever more fluent, productive, and transformative.

Welcome to the hidden world of AI communication. The conversation is about to begin.

Chapter 1: The Birth of Machine Language

Ever tried talking to a brick wall? That's what early computer pioneers faced. They had these amazing machines, but the only language they understood was "on" or "off" – 1s and 0s.

This is the story of machine language, the starting point for everything in computing and AI. It's about how humans learned to speak "machine."

In this chapter, we'll explore how this all began, from the mechanical ideas of Babbage and Lovelace to the first real computers and the languages we used to control them.

Ready to see how we went from brick walls to AI whispers? Let's dive into the birth of machine language!

The Precursors: Early Concepts of Machine Instructions

The story of machine language indeed begins with the groundbreaking work of Ada Lovelace and Charles Babbage in the mid-19th century. Their collaboration on the Analytical Engine laid the foundation for programmable machines and modern computing.

Charles Babbage, often called "the father of computers," designed the Analytical Engine as an automatic digital computer. Although never fully built during their lifetimes, this mechanical marvel was a significant leap forward in computational thinking.

Ada Lovelace, born in 1815, was introduced to Babbage's work in 1833. Her exceptional mathematical skills and unique vision allowed her to see the potential of the Analytical Engine beyond mere calculation.

In 1842-1843, Lovelace translated an article by Italian mathematician Luigi Menabrea about Babbage's Analytical Engine. She added her own extensive notes, which were three times longer than the original article. These notes contained what is now recognized as the first computer program.

Lovelace's most significant contribution was her insight that the Analytical Engine could manipulate symbols according to rules, not just crunch numbers. She wrote that the machine "might act upon other things besides number," suggesting it could potentially compose music or manipulate symbols. This conceptual leap from calculation to computation marked a crucial transition in the history of computing.

In her famous "Note G," Lovelace described an algorithm for the Analytical Engine to compute Bernoulli numbers. This is widely considered the first published algorithm specifically designed for implementation on a computer, earning Lovelace the title of the world's first computer programmer.

Lovelace's work went largely unrecognized until the 1950s, when her notes were republished. Today, she is celebrated as a pioneer in computing, with her contributions acknowledged through various honors, including naming a programming language after her and featuring her on British passports.

The Dawn of Electronic Computing

The dawn of electronic computing marked a revolutionary period in technological history, transforming the landscape of information processing and laying the foundation for our modern digital age.

The First Electronic Computers

The birth of electronic computing can be traced to the late 1930s and early 1940s, with two pioneering machines emerging as the earliest contenders:

1. The Atanasoff-Berry Computer (ABC): Developed between 1937 and 1942 at Iowa State University by John Vincent Atanasoff and Clifford Berry, the ABC introduced several groundbreaking concepts:

    - Parallel processing
    - Separation of memory and computing functions
    - Memory refreshing
    - Binary arithmetic
    - Conversion from base-10 to base-2

2. The Electronic Numerical Integrator and Computer (ENIAC): Created in 1946 by John W. Mauchly and J. Presper Eckert at the University of Pennsylvania. ENIAC was:

    - The first large-scale electronic computer
    - A 30-ton behemoth occupying an entire room
    - Funded by the U.S. Army for artillery firing table calculations

While ENIAC was initially hailed as the first electronic computer, a 1973 U.S. Federal Court ruling officially recognized the ABC as the first.

Wartime Innovations

World War II significantly accelerated computer development:

- Colossus (1943): Built at Bletchley Park, UK, by Alan Turing and colleagues to crack German military codes.
- Z1 (1941): Developed by Konrad Zuse in Germany.

- Mark-1 (1944): Created by Howard Aiken.

Key Technological Advancements

The early computers faced several challenges, which drove further innovations:

- Storage: ENIAC lacked sufficient internal storage for calculations.

- Programming: Changing ENIAC's programs required hours of manual rewiring.

- Binary system: EDVAC (1949) introduced the use of binary numbers for arithmetic operations.

- Internal program storage: EDSAC implemented the ability to store programs internally.

- Parallel operations: The IAS computer introduced simultaneous digit processing.

The Transistor Revolution

In 1948, a breakthrough at Bell Laboratories changed the course of computing. John Bardeen, William Shockley, and Walter Brattain invented the transistor. This solid-state electronic device soon replaced vacuum tubes, allowing for smaller, cooler, and more reliable computers.

Theoretical Foundations

The development of electronic computers was underpinned by crucial theoretical work:

- Alan Turing's 1936 paper on computable numbers laid the groundwork for implementing mathematical logic in machines.

- Claude Shannon's 1948 work provided a theoretical framework for electronic information transmission.

These early innovations in electronic computing set the stage for the rapid development of computer technology and the birth of the computer industry, ushering in a new era of information processing and technological advancement.

Machine Code: The Raw Language of Computers

Machine code, also known as machine language or native code, is the most fundamental language of computers. It consists of binary sequences (0s and 1s) that are directly executed by the computer's central processing unit (CPU). This raw language forms the basis of all computer operations and programming.

Characteristics of Machine Code

- Binary Format: Machine code is expressed solely in binary, using only 0s and 1s.

- Direct Execution: The CPU can understand and execute machine code without any intermediary steps.

- Hardware-Specific: Machine code is tied to specific CPU architectures, meaning code written for one type of processor may not work on another.

- High Performance: Since it's directly executed by the CPU, machine code offers faster processing speeds compared to higher-level languages.

Advantages and Limitations

Advantages:

- Fastest execution speed as it requires no translation6.

- Direct hardware control, crucial for embedded systems and hardware optimization.

Limitations:

- Extremely difficult to write and read for humans.
- Prone to errors due to its complexity.
- Lacks abstraction, requiring explicit description of every operation.
- Machine-dependent, limiting portability across different systems.

Historical Significance

In the early days of computing, programmers had to write operations directly in machine code, a laborious and error-prone process. This necessity drove the development of assembly language and higher-level programming languages to make coding more accessible and efficient.

Modern Applications

While rarely used directly by programmers today, understanding machine code remains crucial for:

- Low-level system programming and optimization.
- Reverse engineering and security analysis.
- Developing embedded systems.
- Understanding the fundamental workings of computers and programming languages.

Assembly Language: The First Step Towards Human-Readable Code

Assembly language marked a significant leap forward in programming, bridging the gap between machine code and human-readable instructions. Developed in the late 1940s, it represented the first step towards making computer programming more accessible and efficient1.

Key Features of Assembly Language

1. Mnemonics: Assembly language uses short, symbolic codes to represent machine instructions. For example:

    - ADD for addition
    - SUB for subtraction
    - MOV for moving data

2. Labels: Symbols representing memory addresses, making it easier to reference specific points in the code.

3. Directives: Instructions for the assembler, not directly translated into machine code.

4. One-to-one correspondence: Generally, each assembly instruction translates to one machine language instruction.

Advantages over Machine Code

1. Readability: Uses alphanumeric commands instead of binary, making it more comprehensible to humans.

2. Error correction: Allows for changes and error corrections, unlike machine code.

3. Standardization: Consists of a standard set of instructions, less platform-dependent than machine code.

Limitations

1. Translation required: An assembler is needed to convert assembly code into machine code.

2. Still low-level: While more readable than machine code, it remains a low-level language requiring detailed hardware knowledge.

3. Performance trade-off: While faster than high-level languages, it's slightly slower in execution compared to pure machine code due to the translation step.

Assembly language played a crucial role in early computing and continues to be used in specific applications like microprocessor-based real-time systems, device drivers, and low-level embedded systems.

The Rise of High-Level Languages

The rise of high-level programming languages marked a revolutionary shift in computer programming, making it more accessible and efficient. This evolution was driven by the increasing complexity of programs and the need for more intuitive ways to communicate with computers.

FORTRAN: The Pioneer

FORTRAN (FORmula TRANslator), developed by John Backus and his team at IBM, emerged as the first widely used high-level programming language16. Key points about FORTRAN include:

- Development began in 1954, with the first manual appearing in October 1956.

- It was officially released in 1957, marking a turning point in computer software.
- FORTRAN allowed programmers to write code in a more natural, formula-like notation.
- It significantly reduced the number of instructions needed for complex calculations.

Impact and Advantages

High-level languages like FORTRAN brought several advantages:

- Abstraction from machine-level details, allowing focus on problem-solving.
- Increased productivity by simplifying the coding process8.
- Improved readability and maintainability of code.
- Greater portability across different computer architectures.

Other Early High-Level Languages

Following FORTRAN's success, several other high-level languages emerged:

- LISP (1958): Designed for artificial intelligence research.
- COBOL (1959): Created for business data processing.
- ALGOL (1958-1960): Introduced important concepts like nested functions and lexical scope.
- BASIC (1964): Developed for students without strong technical backgrounds.

Legacy and Continued Use

High-level languages revolutionized programming, making it accessible to a broader range of professionals. FORTRAN, in particular, remains in use today for scientific and engineering applications, including weather forecasting and genomic simulations.

The rise of high-level languages laid the foundation for modern software development, enabling the creation of increasingly complex and sophisticated computer programs.

Specialized Languages for AI

In the late 1950s, John McCarthy introduced LISP (List Processing), a groundbreaking programming language that revolutionized the field of artificial intelligence. LISP's development marked a crucial milestone in AI history, providing researchers with a powerful tool specifically designed for AI tasks.

Key features of LISP that made it ideal for AI:

- Symbolic Expression Manipulation: LISP's ability to handle symbolic expressions set it apart from other languages of its time. This feature allowed programmers to represent and manipulate complex knowledge structures efficiently.

- Flexibility and Adaptability: LISP's design made it highly flexible, enabling researchers to easily modify and extend the language to suit their specific AI research needs.

- List Processing: As its name suggests, LISP excelled at processing lists, which proved to be a natural way to represent many AI concepts and data structures.

- Metaprogramming: LISP's capacity for metaprogramming, allowing programs to modify themselves during execution, was particularly valuable for developing adaptive AI systems.

LISP quickly became the language of choice for AI research, playing a pivotal role in early AI applications such as:

- Natural Language Processing: LISP's symbolic capabilities made it effective for parsing and understanding human language.

- Automated Reasoning: The language's structure allowed for the encoding of rules and concepts that drive reasoning processes in AI.

- Game-Playing Algorithms: LISP's flexibility supported the development of sophisticated algorithms for strategic decision-making in games.

While LISP's popularity in mainstream programming has declined, its influence on AI and programming language design remains significant. Many modern AI languages and techniques can trace their roots back to concepts first introduced in LISP.

The Evolution of Compilers and Interpreters

The evolution of compilers and interpreters marks a significant milestone in the history of programming languages, bridging the gap between human-readable code and machine-executable instructions.

Early Development

Compilers were developed before interpreters, with the first compiler created by Grace Hopper in 1952. This early compiler translated high-level language code into machine code, creating a standalone executable program4. The development of compilers was driven by the need to simplify programming within the limitations of early computers, such as limited program storage space.

Rise of Interpreters

Interpreters emerged later, with the first interpreted high-level language being Lisp in 1958. Steve Russell implemented the first Lisp interpreter on an IBM 704 computer, realizing that the Lisp eval function could be implemented in machine code.

Key Differences

Compilers translate the entire source code into machine code at once, creating an executable file. Interpreters, on the other hand, translate and execute the source code line by line. This difference allows interpreters to provide more interactive debugging capabilities, while compiled programs generally run faster.

Impact on Programming Efficiency

The development of compilers and interpreters significantly improved programming efficiency:

- Abstraction: Programmers could write code in more abstract, problem-oriented languages.

- Portability: High-level languages became portable between different computer operating systems.

- Debugging: Interpreters made debugging easier by analyzing and checking each line of code before execution.

Modern Applications

Today, compilers and interpreters continue to play crucial roles in software development:

- Cross-platform development: They enable developers to write code once and run it on multiple platforms.

- Just-in-Time (JIT) compilation: Modern systems often combine compilation and interpretation techniques for optimal performance.

The evolution of compilers and interpreters has been fundamental in making programming more accessible and efficient, paving the way for the complex software systems we use today.

The Impact on Early AI Development

The impact of early programming languages, especially LISP, on AI development was profound and far-reaching. LISP's unique features made it particularly well-suited for early AI research and applications.

Symbolic Computation

LISP's ability to manipulate symbolic expressions was revolutionary for AI development. It allowed researchers to represent and process complex knowledge structures efficiently1. This capability was crucial for:

- Natural Language Processing: LISP's symbolic manipulation made it effective for parsing and understanding human language.

- Knowledge Representation: The language's structure allowed for intuitive encoding of concepts and relationships.

Recursive Capabilities

LISP's support for recursive functions was instrumental in solving complex AI problems:

- It enabled efficient implementation of algorithms for tasks like theorem proving and game-playing.

- Recursive functions allowed for elegant solutions to problems involving tree-like data structures, common in AI applications.

Flexibility and Extensibility

LISP's design offered unique advantages for AI research:

- Metaprogramming: LISP's ability to treat code as data allowed for the creation of adaptive AI systems.
- Ecosystem Development: Various dialects and tools emerged, like CLIPS for expert systems, expanding LISP's AI applications\.

Legacy and Continued Influence

While LISP's direct use in modern AI has declined, its impact persists:

- Concepts from LISP have influenced modern AI programming languages and frameworks.
- The symbolic AI approach pioneered with LISP continues to be relevant, with recent research exploring neural-symbolic systems for improved generalization in AI.

LISP's contributions to early AI laid the groundwork for many concepts and techniques still used in AI today, shaping the field's evolution and inspiring new approaches to machine intelligence.

Reflections on the Birth of Machine Language

The journey from binary code to high-level AI languages represents a remarkable evolution in human-machine communication, fundamentally shaping the landscape of computing and artificial intelligence.

The Binary Beginnings

In the early days of computing, programmers worked directly with binary code, laboriously translating their ideas into strings of 1s and 0s1. This process was time-consuming, error-prone, and required an intimate understanding of computer hardware.

The Rise of Assembly Language

Assembly language emerged as the first step towards more human-readable code7. It introduced mnemonics and labels, replacing binary sequences with symbolic representations of instructions. This development significantly improved programming efficiency and reduced errors.

High-Level Languages: A Paradigm Shift

The introduction of high-level languages like FORTRAN in 1957 marked a turning point. These languages allowed programmers to express problems in a more natural, formula-like notation, abstracting away low-level hardware details. This shift enabled programmers to focus on problem-solving rather than machine intricacies.

The Birth of AI-Specific Languages

The development of LISP in 1958 was particularly significant for AI4. LISP's ability to manipulate symbolic expressions made it well-suited for AI tasks, allowing programmers to represent knowledge in ways that closely resembled human thought processes.

Modern AI Languages and Frameworks

Today, we see a diverse ecosystem of languages and frameworks specifically designed for AI development. Python has emerged as a leading language for AI and machine learning, thanks to its simplicity and robust libraries6. Other languages like Julia and Prolog offer specialized capabilities for specific AI applications.

The Ongoing Evolution

As we continue to develop new programming paradigms, we build upon this rich history. The evolution of programming languages has not only made coding more accessible but has also enabled the creation of increasingly sophisticated AI applications.

This journey from binary to high-level AI languages represents more than just technological progress; it reflects our ongoing quest to bridge the gap between human thought and machine execution, constantly seeking more effective ways to communicate with our artificial creations.

Chapter 2: Patterns in the Digital Noise

In the vast ocean of digital information that surrounds us, patterns emerge like constellations in the night sky. These patterns, often invisible to the human eye, hold the key to unlocking the potential of artificial intelligence. Welcome to the world of pattern recognition in AI, where machines learn to see order in chaos and meaning in the seemingly random.

Imagine for a moment that you're standing in front of a massive wall covered in thousands of tiny dots. To the untrained eye, it might appear as nothing more than a chaotic mess. But step back, unfocus your eyes slightly, and suddenly an image emerges – a face, a landscape, or perhaps a complex mathematical equation. This is essentially what AI does when it recognizes patterns, but on a scale and with a precision that far surpasses human capabilities.

Pattern recognition is one of the fundamental techniques that enables machines to identify and classify data patterns. It's the cognitive process that allows AI to sort through vast amounts of information, finding the hidden threads that connect disparate pieces of data. From revolutionizing medical diagnostics to enhancing security systems, pattern recognition is shaping the fluid use of artificial intelligence in ways that touch nearly every aspect of our lives.

In this chapter, we'll explore how AI learns to see these patterns, the techniques it uses to make sense of the digital noise, and the profound impact this capability has on our world. So, let's dive into the fascinating realm where data whispers its secrets to machines, and AI listens with an acuity that continues to astonish and inspire us. Ver tried talking to a brick wall? That's what early computer pioneers faced. They had these amazing machines, but the only language they understood was "on" or "off" – 1s and 0s.

Understanding Pattern Recognition in AI

Pattern recognition is a fundamental concept in artificial intelligence that enables machines to identify and interpret patterns in data. It forms the basis for many AI applications and plays a crucial role in decision-making processes.

Definition and Core Concepts

Pattern recognition is the ability of machines to identify regularities or patterns in data and use these patterns to make decisions or predictions4. It involves analyzing incoming data to detect recurring characteristics or structures that can be used for classification, prediction, or decision-making. The process typically includes data collection, feature extraction, pattern detection, and classification or recognition.

The Role of Pattern Recognition in AI

Pattern recognition is essential in artificial intelligence for several reasons:

- It enables machines to learn from examples and generalize to new situations.
- It forms the basis for many AI applications, including computer vision, speech recognition, and natural language processing.
- It allows AI systems to process and interpret complex data, making it crucial for intelligent decision-making.

Types of Pattern Recognition

There are several approaches to pattern recognition in AI:

- Statistical Pattern Recognition
  This method uses statistical techniques to learn from examples. It involves collecting observations, studying them, and inferring general rules that can be applied to new data. Statistical pattern

recognition is particularly useful in financial applications, such as predicting stock prices based on past market trends.

- Syntactic (Structural) Pattern Recognition
  This approach is used for complex patterns with structural or relational information. It breaks down complex patterns into simpler hierarchical sub-patterns, making it effective for image analysis and natural language processing tasks.

- Neural Pattern Recognition
  Neural networks, particularly deep learning models, are currently the most popular method for pattern detection. They can handle complex, non-linear relationships in data and adapt to new information through training. Neural networks are widely used in computer vision and speech recognition systems.

- Template Matching
  This technique compares input patterns with stored templates to find the best match. It's commonly used in computer vision for object detection, but its effectiveness can be limited when dealing with distorted patterns.

Each of these approaches has its strengths and is suited to different types of pattern recognition tasks. In practice, hybrid approaches that combine multiple methods are often used to leverage the advantages of different techniques

Machine Learning Algorithms for Pattern Recognition

Machine learning algorithms play a crucial role in pattern recognition, enabling AI systems to identify and interpret patterns in data. These algorithms can be broadly categorized into supervised and unsupervised learning approaches.

Supervised Learning Approaches

Supervised learning algorithms learn from labeled training data to make predictions or classifications on new, unseen data. Key supervised learning algorithms for pattern recognition include:

Neural Networks

Neural networks, particularly deep learning models, are highly effective for complex pattern recognition tasks. They consist of interconnected nodes organized in layers, capable of learning hierarchical representations of data. Convolutional Neural Networks (CNNs) are especially powerful for image recognition, while Recurrent Neural Networks (RNNs) excel in sequence-based pattern recognition.

Support Vector Machines (SVMs)

SVMs are effective for both classification and regression tasks. They work by finding the optimal hyperplane that separates different classes in high-dimensional space. SVMs are particularly useful when dealing with non-linearly separable data through the use of kernel functions.

Decision Trees

Decision trees are intuitive algorithms that make decisions based on a series of questions about the input features. Random Forests, an ensemble method using multiple decision trees, are particularly effective for pattern recognition tasks.

Unsupervised Learning Approaches

Unsupervised learning algorithms identify patterns in unlabeled data. Key unsupervised algorithms include:

Clustering Algorithms

K-means clustering and hierarchical clustering are common unsupervised techniques for grouping similar data points together4. These methods can reveal hidden patterns or structures within the data.

Dimensionality Reduction Techniques

Principal Component Analysis (PCA) and t-SNE are used to reduce the dimensionality of data while preserving important patterns and relationships.

Feature Extraction and Selection

Feature extraction and selection are critical steps in pattern recognition:

Feature Extraction

Feature extraction involves transforming raw data into a set of relevant features. Automated methods like autoencoders and wavelet scattering can extract meaningful features from complex data. Deep learning models often perform feature extraction implicitly within their hidden layers.

Feature Selection

Feature selection aims to identify the most relevant features for a given task. This process can improve model performance, reduce overfitting, and enhance interpretability. Common techniques include filter methods, wrapper methods, and embedded methods.

By combining these machine learning algorithms with effective feature extraction and selection techniques, AI systems can achieve high performance in various pattern recognition tasks across industries such as computer vision, natural language processing, and biometric identification.

Image Recognition and Computer Vision

Image recognition and computer vision are fundamental components of modern AI, enabling machines to interpret and analyze visual information. These technologies have revolutionized various fields, from security systems to medical diagnostics.

Fundamentals of Image Processing for Pattern Recognition

Image processing is a crucial step in preparing data for pattern recognition tasks. Key techniques include:

- Image Enhancement: This involves improving image quality by adjusting brightness, contrast, and sharpness.
- Filtering: Used to remove noise or unwanted elements from images, helping to highlight important features.
- Feature Extraction: This process identifies key characteristics in images that are relevant for pattern recognition tasks.

Convolutional Neural Networks (CNNs) and Their Role in Image Analysis

CNNs have become the cornerstone of modern image analysis due to their ability to automatically learn hierarchical features from raw pixel data.

Key aspects of CNNs include:

- Convolutional Layers: These layers apply filters to detect spatial patterns in images.
- Pooling Layers: Used to reduce the spatial dimensions of feature maps, making the network more computationally efficient.
- Fully Connected Layers: These layers interpret the extracted features for final classification or detection tasks.

CNNs excel at tasks such as image classification, object detection, and semantic segmentation due to their ability to capture spatial hierarchies in image data.

Applications

1. Facial Recognition: CNNs can identify and verify individuals in images or video streams with high accuracy.

2. Object Detection: Advanced algorithms like R-CNN, Fast R-CNN, and YOLO can locate and classify multiple objects within a single image.

3. Medical Imaging: Object detection techniques are being applied to various medical imaging modalities:

   - Detecting and classifying breast lesions in mammograms

   - Identifying lung nodules in chest X-rays or CT scans

   - Automating cell counting and localization in pathology slides

These applications are improving diagnostic accuracy and efficiency in healthcare, potentially leading to earlier detection of diseases and improved patient outcomes.

As the field continues to advance, we can expect even more sophisticated applications of image recognition and computer vision across various industries, further bridging the gap between human and machine perception.

Natural Language Processing and Text Analysis

Natural Language Processing (NLP) and text analysis are crucial components of AI that enable machines to understand, interpret, and generate human language. Pattern recognition in textual data forms the foundation of these technologies.

Pattern Recognition in Textual Data

Pattern recognition in textual data involves identifying recurring structures, themes, or relationships within text. Key aspects include:

1. Text Preprocessing: This crucial step prepares raw text for analysis by transforming it into a machine-readable format. It involves:

    - Tokenization: Breaking text into smaller units like words or phrases

    - Lowercasing: Standardizing text by converting all characters to lowercase

    - Stop word removal: Filtering out common words that don't add significant meaning

    - Stemming or lemmatization: Reducing words to their root form

2. Feature Extraction: This process converts preprocessed text into numerical representations. Techniques include:

    - Bag of Words and TF-IDF: Quantifying word presence and importance

    - Word embeddings: Representing words as dense vectors in continuous space

    - Contextual embeddings: Capturing nuanced word meanings based on context

Techniques for Text Classification and Sentiment Analysis

Text classification and sentiment analysis are fundamental NLP tasks that rely heavily on pattern recognition.

1. Text Classification Techniques:
    - Rule-based approaches: These use predefined linguistic rules and patterns.

- Machine learning models: Algorithms learn from data to classify text based on features.

- Deep learning models: Advanced neural networks that can understand context and nuance.

2. Sentiment Analysis Techniques:
   - Rule-based approaches: Rely on predefined rules to determine sentiment.

   - Lexicon-based methods: Count positive and negative words to assign sentiment scores.

   - Machine learning algorithms: Train on labeled data to learn patterns and relationships.

   - Contextual embedding: Uses neural networks to extract complexity and nuance of words.

Language Models and Their Use in Pattern Recognition

Language models play a crucial role in pattern recognition for NLP tasks. They are designed to understand and generate human-like text based on patterns learned from vast amounts of data.

1. Sequence Modeling: Language models like GPT-4 are built on the principle of sequence prediction. They excel at understanding and generating human-like text by predicting the next token in a sequence based on context.

2. Pattern Learning: During training, these models learn complex patterns and relationships within language data. This enables them to bridge the gap between the underlying structure of data and core business concepts.

3. Contextual Understanding: Advanced language models use transformer architecture and self-attention mechanisms to weigh the importance of different parts of the input data. This allows for more nuanced pattern recognition and contextual understanding.

4. Applications: Language models are used in various NLP tasks, including:

   - Machine translation
   - Text summarization
   - Question answering
   - Sentiment analysis
   - Named entity recognition

By leveraging these advanced techniques and models, NLP systems can effectively recognize and interpret complex patterns in textual data, enabling a wide range of applications across industries.

Speech and Audio Pattern Recognition

Speech and audio pattern recognition are fundamental components of modern AI systems, enabling machines to understand and interpret audio signals. This technology has wide-ranging applications, from voice assistants to music identification.

Fundamentals of Speech Recognition Systems

Speech recognition systems typically follow a pipeline consisting of several key components:

- Signal Processing: The system converts spoken words into a digital format that computers can process.

- Feature Extraction: This step filters out background noise and irrelevant information, keeping only critical data for further processing.

- Acoustic Modeling: This component maps extracted features to phonemes, the basic units of sound in a language.

- Language Modeling: This predicts the probability of word sequences, incorporating rules of syntax and grammar.

- Decoding: The final stage combines outputs from acoustic and language models to generate the most probable transcription of the spoken words.

Audio Feature Extraction and Analysis

Audio feature extraction involves transforming raw audio signals into meaningful features for further processing or analysis. Key techniques include:

1. Time Domain Features:

    - Amplitude Envelope: Provides a rough idea of loudness.

    - Root Mean Square Energy: Indicates loudness, less sensitive to outliers than Amplitude Envelope.

    - Zero-Crossing Rate: Useful for music/speech discrimination and voice activity detection.

2. Frequency Domain Features:

- Mel-Frequency Cepstral Coefficients (MFCC): Represent the short-term power spectrum of sound, widely used in speech and audio processing.

- Mel-filterbank Energy (MFE): Focuses on energy in different frequency bands.

3. Time-Frequency Representation:

   - Spectrogram: Combines both time and frequency components of the audio signal.

4. Dimension Reduction Techniques:

   - Principal Component Analysis (PCA)

   - K-means clustering

   - Linear Discriminant Analysis.

Applications in Voice Assistants and Music Identification

1. Voice Assistants:

   - Virtual assistants like Amazon Alexa, Apple's Siri, and Google Home use speech recognition to interpret user commands.

   - These systems employ natural language processing (NLP) to derive meaning from transcribed text and generate appropriate responses.

2. Music Identification:

   - Audio feature extraction techniques are crucial for music identification services.

- Systems can analyze features like spectral centroid, band energy ratio, and spectral bandwidth to identify songs.
- Deep learning approaches using unstructured audio representations like spectrograms have become increasingly popular for music identification tasks.

As speech and audio pattern recognition technologies continue to advance, we can expect even more sophisticated applications across various industries, further bridging the gap between human and machine communication.

Biometric Pattern Recognition

Biometric pattern recognition has become an increasingly important field in security and authentication. This technology leverages unique physical and behavioral characteristics to identify individuals with high accuracy.

Fingerprint and Retinal Scan Technologies

Fingerprint Recognition

Fingerprint scanning is one of the most widely used biometric technologies. It works by capturing and analyzing the unique patterns of ridges and valleys on a person's fingertip. Modern fingerprint scanners can achieve high levels of accuracy, with some smartphone implementations reporting a 1 in 1 million chance of false acceptance.

Retinal Scan Technology

Retinal scanning is an advanced biometric technique that analyzes the unique pattern of blood vessels in a person's retina8. Key features include:

- Uses low-intensity infrared light to illuminate the retina
- Captures an image of the blood vessel pattern
- Converts the image into a digital template for comparison

- Offers extremely high accuracy, with an estimated error rate of one in ten million

Retinal scans are considered one of the most secure biometric methods due to the retina's stability throughout a person's lifetime and the difficulty in replicating or forging retinal patterns.

Behavioral Biometrics

Behavioral biometrics focus on unique patterns in an individual's actions or behaviors.

Gait Analysis

Gait analysis examines an individual's walking pattern. This can include factors like stride length, walking speed, and body movements.

Keystroke Dynamics

Keystroke dynamics analyze typing patterns, including:

- Typing speed
- Pressure applied to keys
- Time between keystrokes
- Common typing errors

These behavioral patterns can create a unique profile for each user, adding an extra layer of security to traditional authentication methods.

Security Applications and Ethical Considerations

Security Applications

Biometric technologies are used across various sectors:

- Government and military: High-security facilities use retinal scanners for access control.

- Border control: Biometrics enhance passport and traveler verification.
- Financial services: Banks use biometrics to secure customer accounts.
- Healthcare: Patient identification ensures correct treatment delivery.
- Mobile devices: Smartphones commonly use fingerprint and facial recognition.

Ethical Considerations

While biometrics offer enhanced security, they also raise important ethical concerns:

- Privacy: The collection and storage of biometric data pose risks if breached or misused.
- Data security: Proper protection of stored biometric information is crucial.
- Consent: Clear guidelines are needed for obtaining and using biometric data.
- Accessibility: Some individuals may be unable to use certain biometric systems due to physical limitations.
- Bias: Biometric systems must be designed and tested to avoid discrimination against certain groups.

As biometric technologies continue to advance, balancing security benefits with ethical considerations will be crucial for widespread adoption and public acceptance.

Pattern Recognition in Big Data and IoT

Pattern recognition in Big Data and IoT environments presents unique challenges and opportunities due to the massive scale and real-time nature of data generated by connected devices. Here's a detailed look at key aspects of pattern recognition in this context:

Handling Large-Scale Data for Pattern Recognition

Big Data generated by IoT devices requires specialized approaches for effective pattern recognition:

- Distributed Computing: Frameworks like Hadoop and Spark enable processing of massive datasets across clusters of computers.

- Dimensionality Reduction: Techniques like Principal Component Analysis (PCA) help reduce data complexity while preserving important patterns.

- Streaming Algorithms: These process data in real-time, updating pattern models incrementally as new data arrives.

- Feature Selection: Identifying the most relevant features from high-dimensional IoT data is crucial for efficient pattern recognition.

Real-Time Pattern Recognition in IoT Devices

IoT devices often require on-device pattern recognition for quick decision-making:

- Edge Computing: Performing pattern recognition directly on IoT devices reduces latency and bandwidth usage.

- Lightweight Algorithms: Resource-constrained IoT devices need efficient algorithms optimized for limited processing power and memory.
- Collaborative Processing: Multiple IoT devices can work together to perform distributed pattern recognition tasks.
- Adaptive Models: Pattern recognition models must adapt to changing conditions and data distributions in IoT environments.

Predictive Maintenance and Anomaly Detection

Pattern recognition plays a crucial role in predictive maintenance and anomaly detection for IoT systems:

- Sensor Data Analysis: IoT sensors provide real-time data on equipment performance, enabling early detection of potential failures.
- Machine Learning Models: Algorithms learn from historical data to predict when maintenance will be needed, reducing unexpected downtime.
- Anomaly Detection: Pattern recognition techniques identify unusual behavior in IoT data streams, flagging potential security threats or system malfunctions.
- Time Series Analysis: Techniques like Fast Fourier Transform (FFT) and Wavelet Transform (WT) extract features from sensor data for anomaly detection.
- Multi-Sensor Fusion: Combining data from multiple IoT sensors (e.g., vibration, temperature, noise) improves the accuracy of predictive maintenance models.

By leveraging these advanced pattern recognition techniques, organizations can extract valuable insights from the vast amounts of data generated by IoT devices, enabling more efficient operations, improved maintenance strategies, and enhanced security in connected systems.

Challenges and Future Directions in AI Pattern Recognition

Pattern recognition in AI continues to evolve rapidly, presenting both challenges and opportunities for future development. Here's a detailed look at the current challenges and emerging directions in this field:

Addressing Bias and Improving Accuracy

Bias in AI pattern recognition systems remains a significant challenge:

- Insufficient or biased training data can lead to poor recognition of underrepresented groups.
- Lack of diversity among programmers designing training samples can contribute to bias.

To mitigate these issues:

- Developers should focus on reducing disparities between groups without sacrificing overall model performance.
- Improving both fairness and accuracy is possible by investigating apparent bugs in the software.
- Additional training data for underrepresented groups can improve accuracy and reduce unfair results.

Emerging Techniques

Transfer Learning

Transfer learning has emerged as a powerful technique for improving pattern recognition:

- It allows models to use knowledge gained from one task to solve similar, new tasks.
- In computer vision, pre-trained models can be fine-tuned to identify specific objects, saving time and effort.
- Models like Ultralytics YOLO can be pre-trained on large datasets and then fine-tuned for specialized tasks.

Few-Shot Learning

Few-shot learning addresses the challenge of limited training data:

- It enables AI systems to learn from just a small number of examples.
- Meta-transfer learning (MTL) has been proposed as a novel few-shot learning method.
- MTL learns to adapt deep neural networks for few-shot learning tasks, improving performance on challenging benchmarks.

The Role of Pattern Recognition in Advancing General AI

Pattern recognition plays a crucial role in the development of more advanced AI systems:

- It forms the foundation for extracting meaningful features and representations from input data.
- Recent advances in AI rely predominantly on machine learning algorithms that discern complex patterns from vast amounts of data.

- Pattern recognition harmonizes with machine learning algorithms, informing the decision-making processes of AI systems.

However, challenges remain:

- Current AI systems excel at pattern recognition but may struggle with genuine creativity that draws on the full range of human experience.

- Continuous model monitoring is necessary to detect and address changes in software or data acquisition that could lead to model failure.

As we move forward, addressing these challenges and leveraging emerging techniques will be crucial for advancing pattern recognition and, by extension, general AI capabilities.

In conclusion, the field of pattern recognition stands at the forefront of artificial intelligence, driving advancements that enhance our interaction with technology and improve decision-making processes across various domains. As we have explored, the integration of sophisticated algorithms, emerging techniques like transfer learning and few-shot learning, and a deeper understanding of the ethical implications surrounding bias are essential for the continued evolution of AI.

Looking ahead, the potential for pattern recognition to contribute to general AI is immense. By refining these systems and ensuring they are robust, fair, and adaptable, we can unlock new possibilities for innovation. As we continue to navigate the complexities of data in an increasingly interconnected world, the ability to recognize and interpret patterns will remain a cornerstone of AI development, shaping the future of technology and its role in our lives.

Chapter 3: When AIs Talk to Each Other

As artificial intelligence continues to evolve, the ability for AIs to communicate and collaborate with one another is becoming increasingly vital. This chapter delves into the fascinating world of AI-to-AI communication, where intelligent systems not only process information independently but also engage in dialogue, share insights, and work together to tackle complex challenges. Just as humans rely on collaboration to solve problems and innovate, AIs are beginning to form their own networks of interaction, paving the way for unprecedented advancements across various domains.

Imagine a fleet of autonomous vehicles seamlessly exchanging data about traffic conditions, hazards, and optimal routes in real time. Picture smart grids that intelligently coordinate energy distribution based on consumption patterns and renewable energy availability. These scenarios exemplify the immense potential of AI-to-AI communication, where systems leverage collective intelligence to enhance efficiency, safety, and decision-making. In this chapter, we will explore the mechanisms behind AI communication, the applications that benefit from this collaboration, and the future implications of interconnected intelligent systems.

Fundamentals of AI-to-AI Communication

AI-to-AI communication is a crucial aspect of modern artificial intelligence systems, enabling them to exchange information and collaborate effectively. This communication relies on specific protocols, standards, and data exchange formats to ensure seamless interaction between different AI systems.

Protocols and Standards for AI Communication

AI systems utilize various protocols and standards to facilitate communication:

1. Web APIs: These are commonly used for AI-to-AI communication, including:
    - REST (Representational State Transfer) APIs: Use HTTP requests for data exchange.
    - SOAP (Simple Object Access Protocol) APIs: Employ XML-based messaging for structured information exchange.
    - GraphQL APIs: Allow clients to request specific data, reducing network traffic.
2. Remote Procedure Call (RPC) APIs: Enable direct function calls between AI systems, with gRPC being a high-performance example.
3. Event-Driven APIs: Facilitate real-time information exchange between AI systems:
    - Webhooks: Deliver data to other applications as events occur.
    - Pub/Sub (Publish/Subscribe) APIs: Used in event-driven architectures for message distribution.
4. Streaming APIs: Enable real-time data exchange, with WebSockets providing full-duplex communication channels.

Data Exchange Formats and APIs

AI systems use various data exchange formats to ensure efficient communication:

1. JSON (JavaScript Object Notation): A lightweight, human-readable format widely used in web services.

2. XML (eXtensible Markup Language): Offers a structured format for data exchange, often used in SOAP APIs.

3. CSV (Comma-Separated Values): A simple format for tabular data exchange.

4. Protocol Buffers: A binary serialization format used in gRPC for efficient data transfer.

APIs play a crucial role in facilitating AI-to-AI communication, providing standardized interfaces for data exchange and function calls between systems.

Challenges in Ensuring Interoperability Between AI Systems

Interoperability remains a significant challenge in AI-to-AI communication:

1. Data Security and Privacy: Ensuring secure data transfer while maintaining integrity and confidentiality is crucial.

2. Standardization: The lack of universal standards for AI communication can lead to compatibility issues between different systems.

3. Data Quality: Incomplete or inaccurate data can hinder effective communication and lead to errors in AI decision-making.

4. Regulatory Compliance: Diverse AI governance approaches across jurisdictions can create challenges in achieving regulatory interoperability.

5. Technical Specification Conflicts: Different requirements for technical specifications can impede seamless communication between AI systems.

To address these challenges, efforts are being made to develop regulatory interoperability and harmonization across different jurisdictions. Additionally, technologies like Natural Language Processing (NLP) are being employed to improve data quality and facilitate better communication between AI systems

Applications of AI-to-AI Communication

AI-to-AI communication is revolutionizing various industries by enabling intelligent systems to collaborate and share information efficiently. Here's a detailed look at some key applications:

Autonomous Vehicle Networks and Traffic Management

Autonomous vehicles leverage AI-to-AI communication to enhance safety and optimize traffic flow:

- Real-time data exchange: Vehicles share information about road conditions, accidents, and traffic patterns.
- Coordinated movement: AI systems in different vehicles communicate to maintain safe distances and coordinate lane changes.
- Traffic light optimization: AI-powered traffic management systems adjust signal timings based on real-time vehicle data to reduce congestion.

Smart Grid Optimization and Energy Distribution

AI communication is transforming energy management in smart grids:

- Real-time monitoring and automation: AI systems continuously analyze data from sensors and smart meters to monitor grid health and identify potential issues.

- Demand response: AI algorithms predict demand surges or drops, enabling proactive management of electricity consumption.

- Renewable energy integration: AI helps grid operators integrate variable renewable energy sources more effectively by accurately predicting energy production.

Supply Chain and Logistics Coordination

AI-to-AI communication streamlines supply chain operations:

- Inventory management: AI systems communicate to optimize stock levels across multiple locations.

- Route optimization: AI-powered logistics systems exchange data to determine the most efficient delivery routes.

- Demand forecasting: AI algorithms share market insights to improve production and distribution planning.

Financial Trading Systems

AI communication is reshaping financial markets:

- Multi-agent systems: Frameworks like TradingAgents simulate real-world trading firms using specialized AI agents for different roles.

- Real-time data analysis: AI trading systems process market data continuously, enabling instant reactions to changing conditions.

- Algorithmic trading: AI-powered algorithms analyze past data, evaluate market conditions, and adjust trading strategies to optimize returns.

These applications demonstrate how AI-to-AI communication is enhancing efficiency, decision-making, and automation across various sectors, paving the way for more intelligent and interconnected systems.

Collaborative Problem-Solving Among AIs

Collaborative problem-solving among AIs is an emerging field that leverages the collective capabilities of multiple AI systems to tackle complex challenges. This approach has led to significant advancements in distributed computing, swarm intelligence, and privacy-preserving machine learning techniques.

Distributed AI Systems for Complex Computations

Distributed AI systems enable the processing of large-scale computational tasks by dividing them across multiple machines:

- These systems are particularly useful for training deep learning models, which often require extensive computational resources.

- By distributing the training process across multiple nodes, each working on a portion of the data, the overall training time is significantly reduced.

- This approach allows for the development of more complex models that can handle larger networks than a single machine could process.

Swarm Intelligence and Multi-Agent Systems

Swarm intelligence applies the principles of collective behavior observed in nature to AI systems:

- In multi-agent systems, swarm intelligence enhances problem-solving and decision-making capabilities through simple rules that agents follow.

- Practical applications include robotic swarms, where groups of drones can collaborate for tasks like search and rescue or environmental monitoring.

- Traffic management systems also benefit from swarm intelligence, with connected vehicles sharing real-time data to optimize routes and reduce congestion.

Multi-agent systems (MAS) consist of multiple autonomous agents interacting within a shared environment:

- These systems offer advantages such as robustness, scalability, and adaptability.

- MAS can handle dynamic, unpredictable situations with remarkable flexibility due to their decentralized nature6.

- Applications of MAS range from traffic management and disaster response to online marketplaces with trading agents6.

Federated Learning for Privacy-Preserving Collaboration

Federated learning is an innovative approach that allows AI models to learn from decentralized data sources while preserving privacy:

- This technique enables multiple parties to collaboratively train a model without sharing raw data.

- It's particularly useful in scenarios where data privacy is crucial, such as healthcare or financial services.

- Federated learning allows for the development of more robust and generalizable models by leveraging diverse datasets from multiple sources.

As collaborative problem-solving among AIs continues to evolve, platforms like SmythOS are emerging to facilitate the development and deployment of sophisticated multi-agent systems. These platforms offer features such as real-time monitoring, event-based triggers, and seamless API integration, enabling developers to create more adaptive and efficient autonomous systems

AI Communication in IoT Ecosystems

AI communication within IoT ecosystems enables connected devices to process, share, and act on data collaboratively. This synergy between AI and IoT enhances efficiency, decision-making, and automation across various domains. Below is a detailed exploration of key aspects:

Edge Computing and AI Coordination in IoT Networks

Edge computing plays a pivotal role in optimizing AI-IoT communication by processing data closer to its source:

- Real-Time Decision-Making: Edge computing reduces latency by enabling IoT devices to analyze data locally rather than relying on centralized cloud systems. For example, cooling systems in industrial environments can be activated instantly when edge devices detect overheating.

- Bandwidth Optimization: By filtering and preprocessing data at the edge, only essential information is sent to the cloud for long-term storage or further analysis, reducing network congestion.

- AI at the Edge: Advanced edge devices equipped with AI models (e.g., NVIDIA Jetson hardware) can perform inference tasks like real-time anomaly detection or predictive maintenance without requiring high computational resources.

This localized processing enhances responsiveness and enables IoT systems to function autonomously in critical applications such as industrial automation, healthcare monitoring, and smart cities.

Smart Home Device Interactions and Automation

In smart home ecosystems, AI communication enables seamless interaction between devices for enhanced automation:

- Device Interoperability: Smart home devices like thermostats, lighting systems, and security cameras communicate using protocols such as Zigbee or Wi-Fi. AI algorithms analyze user behavior patterns to automate tasks like adjusting temperature or turning off lights when no one is home.

- Voice Assistants: AI-powered assistants (e.g., Amazon Alexa or Google Assistant) act as hubs for smart home communication, coordinating actions across multiple devices based on voice commands or pre-set routines.

- Energy Efficiency: Smart meters and appliances use AI to optimize energy consumption by analyzing usage patterns and recommending adjustments to reduce waste.

This interconnectedness creates a personalized and efficient living environment while minimizing manual intervention.

Industrial IoT (IIoT) and AI-Driven Process Optimization

AI communication within IIoT networks transforms manufacturing and industrial operations through process optimization:

- Predictive Maintenance: IoT sensors continuously monitor machinery for early signs of wear or failure. AI algorithms analyze this data to predict maintenance needs, reducing downtime and extending equipment lifespan.

- Real-Time Process Adjustments: AI systems dynamically adjust production parameters based on sensor feedback to minimize waste and maximize efficiency. For instance, generative AI can automate the programming of robotic systems for complex tasks.
- Supply Chain Optimization: IIoT networks enable real-time tracking of inventory levels, shipment statuses, and demand forecasts. AI algorithms coordinate these data streams to optimize logistics and prevent bottlenecks.

By integrating AI with IIoT, industries achieve greater operational efficiency, cost savings, and adaptability in response to changing demands.

AI communication within IoT ecosystems is unlocking new possibilities across residential, industrial, and commercial domains. From real-time decision-making at the edge to seamless device interactions in smart homes and transformative process optimization in industries, this synergy is driving innovation while addressing challenges like latency, bandwidth constraints, and scalability. As these technologies continue to evolve, their impact will further redefine how we interact with connected systems.

Security and Privacy in AI-to-AI Communication

Security and privacy are critical concerns in AI-to-AI communication, as these systems often handle sensitive data and make important decisions. Here's a detailed look at key aspects of security and privacy in AI-to-AI communication:

Encryption and Secure Data Exchange Between AI Systems

Encryption is essential for protecting data exchanged between AI systems:

- AI systems should use strong encryption protocols to secure data both in transit and at rest.

- Secure APIs, such as those using HTTPS, should be implemented for data exchange between AI systems.

- Edge computing can enhance security by processing sensitive data locally, reducing the need to transmit it over networks.

Preventing Adversarial Attacks in AI Networks

Adversarial attacks pose a significant threat to AI systems. To mitigate these risks:

- Implement robust model training using diverse, high-quality data and regularly update models to adapt to evolving threats.

- Use adversarial training techniques, such as the Fast Gradient Sign Method (FGSM), to strengthen models against potential attacks.

- Deploy continuous monitoring systems to detect anomalies or unexpected behavior in AI models.

- Employ ensemble methods and diverse model architectures to make attacks more challenging.

Ethical Considerations in AI Collaboration

As AI systems collaborate, ethical considerations become increasingly important:

- Ensure transparency in AI decision-making processes through the use of Explainable AI (XAI) techniques.

- Implement human oversight in AI collaboration, especially for decisions that may have significant impacts on individuals.

- Regularly assess and mitigate potential biases in AI systems to ensure fairness and inclusivity.

- Clearly communicate the use of AI systems to users, including any limitations in accuracy or potential risks.

By addressing these security, privacy, and ethical considerations, organizations can foster more responsible and trustworthy AI-to-AI communication systems.

Future Directions in AI-to-AI Interaction

The future of AI-to-AI interaction is rapidly evolving, with emerging standards, collaborative innovation, and scaling challenges shaping its trajectory. Here's a detailed look at the key aspects:

Emerging Standards for AI Communication

Standards are crucial for ensuring interoperability and responsible AI development:

- AS ISO/IEC 42001:2023, recently adopted by Standards Australia, provides a framework for AI management systems. This standard addresses unique AI challenges like ethical considerations and transparency, supporting responsible AI development across organizations.

- The European Union's AI Act, set to come into force, is dubbed 'the world's first comprehensive AI law'. This legislation will likely influence global standards for AI communication and deployment.

Potential for AI-Driven Innovation Through Collaboration

AI-to-AI collaboration is opening new frontiers for innovation:

- Multimodal AI systems are emerging as game-changers, integrating text, voice, visuals, and data simultaneously. By 2034, these systems are expected to power advanced virtual assistants and chatbots capable of understanding complex queries and providing tailored responses.

- API-driven AI and microservices will enable businesses to integrate advanced AI functions modularly, speeding up innovation cycles. This approach allows for faster development of custom applications without extensive AI expertise.

- The concept of a distributed "Internet of AI" or federated AI is being developed. This decentralized AI infrastructure could enhance privacy and reduce latency by processing data locally across multiple devices and locations.

Challenges and Opportunities in Scaling AI-to-AI Systems

Scaling AI-to-AI systems presents both challenges and opportunities:

- Computational complexity is a significant challenge, particularly in transformer architectures. Researchers are exploring ways to linearize attention mechanisms or introduce more efficient windowing techniques to handle larger context windows without exponential increases in computational resources.

- Neuromorphic computing, which mimics the neural structure of the human brain, is at the forefront of addressing computational challenges in AI. This approach could lead to more efficient and scalable AI systems.

- Ethical considerations and bias mitigation remain crucial as AI systems scale. Guidelines for AI use in communications and other sectors emphasize the importance of transparency, accuracy, fairness, and privacy protection.

As AI-to-AI interaction continues to advance, it promises to enhance productivity, drive innovation, and tackle complex challenges across industries. However, responsible development and deployment, guided by emerging standards and ethical considerations, will be crucial to realizing its full potential.

In conclusion, the evolution of AI-to-AI communication represents a transformative shift in how intelligent systems interact and collaborate. As we have explored throughout this chapter, the integration of emerging standards, innovative frameworks, and collaborative approaches is paving the way for unprecedented advancements across various sectors. From autonomous vehicles to smart grids, the potential applications are vast and varied, demonstrating the power of interconnected AI systems working together to solve complex problems.

However, as we embrace this future, it is essential to remain vigilant about the challenges that accompany AI-to-AI interaction. Ensuring security, privacy, and ethical considerations must be at the forefront of our efforts to build robust and trustworthy systems. By addressing these concerns and fostering a culture of responsible AI development, we can unlock the full potential of AI-to-AI communication, driving innovation and creating a more efficient and interconnected world. As we look ahead, the collaboration between AI systems will undoubtedly shape the future of technology, making it imperative for researchers, developers, and policymakers to work together in navigating this exciting frontier.

Chapter 4: Decoding AI Decision Trees

In the intricate world of artificial intelligence, decision-making processes form the backbone of intelligent systems. At the heart of many AI applications lies a powerful and intuitive concept: the decision tree. This chapter delves into the fascinating realm of AI decision trees, unraveling the mechanisms that enable machines to make choices, classify data, and predict outcomes with remarkable accuracy.

Decision trees in AI mirror the human decision-making process in many ways, breaking down complex problems into a series of simpler, manageable decisions. Like a flowchart of choices, these trees guide an AI system through a maze of data, leading to conclusions based on learned patterns and predefined rules. As we explore the inner workings of decision trees, we'll uncover how they transform raw data into actionable insights, powering applications across diverse fields from finance to healthcare, marketing to environmental science.

In this chapter, we'll journey through the forest of AI decision-making, examining the roots of these powerful algorithms, their growth into sophisticated models, and the fruits they bear in real-world applications. We'll also confront the challenges and ethical considerations that arise as we entrust more of our decision-making processes to artificial intelligence. Join us as we decode the logic behind AI decision trees and uncover the potential, they hold for shaping our future.

Foundations of AI Decision-Making

AI decision-making processes form the foundation of intelligent systems that can analyze data, identify patterns, and make informed choices. These processes rely on sophisticated algorithms and data analysis techniques to transform raw information into actionable insights.

Introduction to AI Decision-Making Processes

AI decision-making processes involve several key steps:

1. Data Collection: Gathering relevant information from various sources.

2. Data Preprocessing: Cleaning and preparing data for analysis.

3. Feature Extraction: Identifying important attributes in the data.

4. Model Training: Using algorithms to learn patterns from historical data.

5. Prediction/Classification: Applying trained models to new data.

6. Decision Output: Generating actionable recommendations or choices.

These processes enable AI systems to handle complex tasks and make decisions with a level of accuracy and speed that often surpasses human capabilities.

The Role of Algorithms in AI Decision Systems

Algorithms are the backbone of AI decision systems, providing the logical framework for processing data and making choices. Key types of algorithms include:

1. Machine Learning Algorithms: These learn from data to improve performance over time without explicit programming.

2. Deep Learning and Neural Networks: Mimicking the human brain, these analyze complex datasets for pattern recognition.

3. Natural Language Processing (NLP): Enabling machines to understand and interpret human language.

4. Support Vector Machines (SVM): Effective for classification and regression in high-dimensional spaces.

These algorithms work together to process information, perform logical reasoning, and apply mathematical skills to make informed decisions.

Data Analysis Techniques for Informed Decision-Making

AI leverages various data analysis techniques to extract meaningful insights:

1. Predictive Analytics: Using historical data to forecast future trends and outcomes.

2. Regression Analysis: Predicting continuous outcomes based on input variables.

3. Time Series Analysis: Analyzing sequential data to identify trends over time.

4. Clustering: Grouping similar data points to uncover hidden patterns.

5. Ensemble Methods: Combining multiple models to improve prediction accuracy.

These techniques enable AI systems to process large volumes of complex data efficiently, transforming raw information into valuable insights that drive smarter decision-making.

By integrating these foundations - AI decision-making processes, sophisticated algorithms, and advanced data analysis techniques - organizations can harness the power of AI to enhance their decision-making capabilities, leading to improved operational efficiency and strategic outcomes.

Understanding Decision Trees in AI

Decision trees are powerful tools in AI that model decision-making processes through a tree-like structure. They are widely used for both classification and regression tasks, offering interpretability and the ability to handle various data types.

Concept and Structure of Decision Trees

A decision tree consists of three main elements:

1. Root Node: The starting point containing the overarching question or decision.

2. Branches: Representing options, criteria, or courses of action.

3. Leaf Nodes: Representing outcomes, further questions, or probabilities.

The tree structure starts with a root node and branches out based on feature evaluations, forming internal nodes (decision nodes) and ultimately leading to leaf nodes that represent final outcomes or predictions.

Types of Decision Trees: Classification and Regression Trees

There are two primary types of decision trees:

1. Classification Trees: Used to group and categorize data into discrete classes or categories. For example, determining whether a student should study on campus or online based on various attributes.

2. Regression Trees: Used to predict continuous values or estimate real numbers. For instance, calculating the overall benefit of further study, including intangible benefits and potential future opportunities.

Both types employ a top-down, recursive approach to split data and make predictions.

Advantages and Limitations of Decision Tree Models

Advantages:

1. Interpretability: Easy to understand and explain, making them suitable for transparent decision-making.

2. Nonlinear Relationships: Can capture complex, nonlinear relationships between features and target variables.

3. Feature Importance: Provide insights into the relative importance of different features for predictions.

Limitations:

1. Overfitting: Can easily overfit the training data if not properly pruned or limited in depth.

2. Instability: Small changes in training data can lead to significantly different tree structures.

3. Limited Expressiveness: A single tree might not capture complex relationships present in the data.

4. Bias towards Features with Many Levels: May favor features with numerous levels over those with fewer levels.

To address these limitations, ensemble methods like Random Forests and Gradient Boosting have been developed, combining multiple decision trees to improve performance and robustness

Building and Optimizing Decision Trees

Building and optimizing decision trees involves several key steps, from data preparation to model refinement. Here's a detailed look at the process:

Feature Selection and Data Preprocessing

Feature selection is crucial for building effective decision trees:

- Relevance: Select features that are most relevant to the target variable.
- Dimensionality Reduction: Remove redundant or irrelevant features to improve model performance and reduce overfitting.
- Data Cleaning: Handle missing values and outliers to ensure data quality.

While decision trees can naturally select important features, preprocessing can still be beneficial, especially for large datasets, as it can speed up the fitting procedure.

Tree Construction Algorithms

Several algorithms are used to construct decision trees:

- ID3 (Iterative Dichotomiser 3): Uses information gain to select the best feature for splitting.
- C4.5: An improvement over ID3, handling both continuous and discrete attributes.
- CART (Classification and Regression Trees): Supports both classification and regression tasks, using Gini impurity for splits.

These algorithms work by recursively splitting the data based on the feature that provides the most information gain or reduction in impurity.

Pruning Techniques and Handling Overfitting

Decision trees are prone to overfitting, especially when allowed to grow to their full depth. Pruning is a crucial technique to mitigate this issue:

1. Pre-pruning:
   - Set hyperparameters like max_depth, min_samples_leaf, and min_samples_split to limit tree growth.
   - Monitor cross-validation error during tree building and stop when it no longer decreases.
2. Post-pruning:
   - Allow the tree to grow fully, then remove branches that don't improve performance.
   - Cost Complexity Pruning (CCP) is a common technique, controlled by the ccp_alpha parameter.
3. Reduced Error Pruning (REP):
   - Replace nodes with their most popular class if prediction accuracy is not affected.
   - Simple and fast method for pruning.
4. Cost Complexity Pruning (CCP):
   - Generates a series of trees, progressively removing subtrees.

- Chooses the best tree based on a balance between complexity and error rate.

By employing these techniques, decision trees can be optimized to provide better generalization and avoid overfitting, leading to more robust and accurate models.

Advanced Decision Tree Techniques

Advanced decision tree techniques have significantly improved the performance and capabilities of tree-based models in machine learning. These methods address many limitations of single decision trees by leveraging ensemble approaches and sophisticated algorithms.

Random Forests and Ensemble Methods

Random Forests are a powerful ensemble learning method that combines multiple decision trees to create a more robust and accurate model:

- They create numerous decision trees using random subsets of the training data and features.

- For classification tasks, the final prediction is determined by majority voting among all trees.

- In regression problems, the average prediction of all trees is used as the final output.

Random Forests offer several advantages:

- Reduced overfitting compared to single decision trees

- Ability to handle high-dimensional data effectively

- Robustness against missing data

Gradient Boosting Decision Trees (GBDT)

Gradient Boosting is an iterative technique that builds a strong predictive model by combining multiple weak learners, typically decision trees:

- It works by sequentially adding new models to correct the errors of the existing ensemble.
- Each new tree is trained to predict the residuals or errors of the previous models.
- The final prediction is the sum of all tree predictions, weighted to minimize the loss function.

Key features of GBDT include:

- High predictive accuracy
- Ability to handle complex, nonlinear relationships in data
- Flexibility in loss function selection

XGBoost and LightGBM Algorithms

XGBoost (Extreme Gradient Boosting) and LightGBM are advanced implementations of gradient boosting that offer improved performance and efficiency:

XGBoost:

- Uses a more regularized model formalization to control overfitting
- Implements parallel processing for faster computation
- Handles sparse data efficiently

LightGBM:

- Uses histogram-based algorithms for faster training
- Implements leaf-wise tree growth instead of level-wise, potentially leading to better accuracy
- Supports efficient handling of categorical features

Both XGBoost and LightGBM have gained popularity in machine learning competitions and real-world applications due to their high performance and scalability.

These advanced decision tree techniques have significantly expanded the capabilities of tree-based models, making them powerful tools for a wide range of machine learning tasks.

Interpretability and Explainable AI

Interpretability and explainable AI are crucial aspects of modern machine learning systems, particularly for decision trees. These concepts enable users to understand how AI models make decisions and provide transparency in the decision-making process.

Importance of Interpretable AI Models

Interpretable AI models are essential for several reasons:

- Establishing trust: Transparent decision-making processes help build confidence among stakeholders, clients, and end-users.
- Legal and ethical considerations: Interpretability allows organizations to account for potential harm and explain decisions, addressing privacy and fairness concerns.

- Debugging and troubleshooting: Understanding model behavior facilitates identifying and correcting errors or biases.
- Regulatory compliance: Many industries require transparency in AI decision-making processes.

Techniques for Visualizing Decision Trees

Several methods can be used to visualize decision trees:

- Scikit-learn's tree.plot_tree(): Provides a basic visualization of the tree structure.
- Graphviz: Offers more customizable tree visualizations.
- dtreeviz package: Provides detailed visualizations including feature distributions and class distributions in nodes.
- SuperTree package: Offers interactive visualizations with features like dragging, zooming, and node collapsing.

Example code for dtreeviz visualization:

```
python
from dtreeviz.trees import dtreeviz

viz = dtreeviz(clf, X, y,
          target_name="target",
          feature_names=feature_names,
          class_names=class_names)
viz.save("decision_tree.svg")
```

Extracting Rules and Insights from Decision Trees

Extracting rules from decision trees helps in understanding the model's decision-making process:

- For classification tasks, rules can be extracted by traversing the tree from root to leaf nodes.
- For regression tasks, rules can be extracted similarly, with leaf nodes representing predicted values instead of classes.

Example of extracted rules for a regression task:

```
python
from sklearn.tree import DecisionTreeRegressor

regr = DecisionTreeRegressor(max_depth=3, random_state=1234)
model = regr.fit(X, y)

rules = get_rules(regr, feature_names, None)
for r in rules:
    print(r)
```

These techniques enable better interpretation of decision tree models, allowing users to understand the logic behind predictions and make informed decisions based on the model's output.

Real-World Applications of AI Decision Trees

AI decision trees have found widespread applications across various sectors, demonstrating their versatility and effectiveness in real-world scenarios:

Financial Sector: Credit Scoring and Fraud Detection

Decision trees play a crucial role in financial services:

- Credit Scoring: Banks use decision trees to evaluate loan applications based on factors like income, credit history, and employment status. This approach ensures fair and consistent lending decisions.

- Fraud Detection: AI-driven Fraud Detection Systems (FDS) in banking leverage decision trees, particularly Gradient Boosting Decision Trees (GBDT), to provide real-time detection and prevention across multiple channels, including mobile apps and online banking.

Healthcare: Diagnosis Support and Treatment Planning

In healthcare, decision trees assist in various aspects of patient care:

- Diagnosis Support: Doctors apply decision trees to diagnose diseases based on symptoms. For example, a decision tree might start with fever as the root node and branch out to various illnesses.

- Treatment Planning: AI algorithms, including decision trees, evaluate multiple potential diagnoses and treatment options, presenting the most effective ones based on the patient's unique profile3. This enables the development of highly tailored treatment plans that suit individual patient needs.

Marketing: Customer Segmentation and Targeted Advertising

Decision trees are widely used in marketing for:

- Customer Segmentation: Marketing teams categorize customers based on demographics, buying habits, and preferences. This segmentation enables businesses to tailor their strategies and boost customer retention.

- Targeted Advertising: By analyzing customer data, decision trees can determine which channels are most likely to yield the highest conversion rates, allowing for more efficient allocation of marketing budgets.

Environmental Science: Species Classification and Habitat Modeling

In environmental science, decision trees contribute to:

- Species Classification: Decision trees can be used to classify different species based on their characteristics, aiding in biodiversity studies.

- Habitat Modeling: By analyzing environmental factors, decision trees can predict suitable habitats for various species, supporting conservation efforts.

These applications demonstrate the power of AI decision trees in transforming data into actionable insights across diverse fields, from financial risk assessment to environmental conservation.

Ethical Considerations in AI Decision-Making

Ethical considerations in AI decision-making are crucial for ensuring responsible and fair use of artificial intelligence. Here's a detailed look at key aspects:

Bias Detection and Mitigation in Decision Tree Models

Bias in AI models, including decision trees, can lead to unfair outcomes:

- Detection: Techniques like measuring correlations between model errors and protected attributes can identify bias.

- Mitigation: Modifying loss functions with regularization terms can penalize high correlations between errors and protected attributes.

- Implementation: This approach has been applied to random forest, gradient-boosted, and XGBoost models, showing improvements in fairness without significant accuracy loss.

Fairness and Transparency in AI Decision Systems

Ensuring fairness and transparency is essential for building trust in AI systems:

- Fairness: AI systems should treat all individuals equally, avoiding discrimination based on protected characteristics like race or gender.

- Transparency: AI decision-making processes should be understandable and explainable, allowing stakeholders to comprehend how decisions are made.

- Explainable AI: Techniques that make AI models more interpretable, such as visualizing decision trees, can enhance transparency.

Regulatory Compliance and Responsible AI Practices

Organizations must adhere to regulations and implement responsible AI practices:

- Governance Frameworks: Establishing robust governance models and regulatory frameworks is crucial for responsible AI use.

- Regular Audits: Conducting regular assessments helps evaluate AI system performance and compliance.

- Compliance Monitoring: Implementing AI TRISM (Trust, Risk, and Security Management) can integrate ethical oversight into deployment pipelines8.

- Human Oversight: Keeping humans in the loop allows for intervention when AI systems produce questionable results9.

By addressing these ethical considerations, organizations can develop AI decision-making systems that are fair, transparent, and compliant with regulations, fostering trust and ensuring responsible use of AI technology.

Future Trends in AI Decision-Making

The future of AI decision-making is evolving rapidly, with several key trends shaping its trajectory:

Integration with Other AI Techniques

Decision trees are increasingly being integrated with other AI techniques, particularly neural networks:

- Neuro-symbolic AI: This approach combines the logical reasoning of symbolic AI with the pattern recognition capabilities of neural networks. For example, in autonomous vehicles, neural networks process visual data while symbolic reasoning applies traffic laws and safety protocols.

- GRU-Tree: This hybrid model applies a regularized tree algorithm to a Gated Recurrent Unit (GRU) neural network, making complex time-series predictions more interpretable. This could be particularly useful in financial forecasting.

Adaptive and Online Decision Tree Learning

Advancements in online and adaptive decision tree learning are enhancing the efficiency and applicability of these models:

- Active Feature Acquisition: New frameworks like UFODT (Utility of Features for Online learning of Decision Trees) are being developed to construct online decision trees more efficiently. This approach requires fewer data points to learn effectively and incurs lower costs for label prediction.

- Posterior Sampling: This technique is being employed in online learning models to improve regret guarantees in canonical online learning settings.

The Role of Decision Trees in Explainable AI Frameworks

Decision trees continue to play a crucial role in explainable AI:

- Transparency in AI Systems: Decision trees enhance the interpretability of AI models by providing clear insights into the decision-making process. This is particularly important in fields like finance and healthcare where understanding the reasoning behind AI decisions is critical.

- Feature Importance: Decision trees can quantify feature importance through metrics like 'gain', offering both global and local perspectives on which features most influence decisions.

- Transforming Complex Models: There's a growing trend of transforming complex AI models into decision trees to make them more interpretable. This approach allows for the benefits of sophisticated AI while maintaining explainability.

As AI continues to advance, these trends in decision tree technology will likely play a significant role in shaping the future of AI decision-making, particularly in areas where transparency and interpretability are paramount.

In conclusion, the exploration of AI decision trees reveals their profound impact on various domains, from finance and healthcare to marketing and environmental science. As we have discussed throughout this chapter, decision trees not only provide a robust framework for decision-making but also enhance interpretability and transparency in AI systems. Their ability to model complex relationships while remaining accessible to users makes them invaluable tools in the evolving landscape of artificial intelligence.

Looking ahead, the integration of decision trees with other AI techniques, advancements in adaptive learning, and their pivotal role in explainable AI frameworks will continue to shape their relevance and application. As organizations strive for more responsible and ethical AI practices, understanding and mitigating bias, ensuring fairness, and adhering to regulatory standards will be essential. By embracing these principles, we can harness the full potential of decision trees while fostering trust and accountability in AI decision-making processes.

As we move forward into an era increasingly defined by intelligent systems, the insights gained from this chapter will serve as a foundation for leveraging decision trees effectively. By continuing to innovate and refine these models, we can unlock new opportunities for enhancing decision-making across diverse fields, ultimately leading to more informed choices that benefit society as a whole.

Chapter 5: The Ethics of Machine Murmurs

As artificial intelligence continues to weave itself into the fabric of our daily lives, we find ourselves at a critical juncture where the whispers of machines are growing louder, influencing decisions that shape our world. This chapter delves into the ethical labyrinth of AI communication and decision-making, exploring the profound implications of entrusting increasingly complex choices to algorithms and machine learning systems. We stand on the precipice of a new era, where the lines between human and artificial intelligence blur, raising fundamental questions about fairness, transparency, and accountability.

In the pages that follow, we will navigate the murky waters of AI ethics, examining the potential biases that lurk within algorithms and their far-reaching consequences on individuals and society. We will confront the challenges of ensuring that AI systems remain accountable for their actions and decisions, even as they grow more autonomous and sophisticated. As we unravel these ethical dilemmas, we must grapple with a central question: How can we harness the immense potential of AI while safeguarding the values and principles that define our humanity?

Foundations of AI Ethics

Key Ethical Principles in AI Development and Deployment

Several fundamental ethical principles guide AI development and deployment:

5. Fairness and Non-discrimination: AI systems must treat all individuals equitably, regardless of protected characteristics like race, gender, or age.

6. Transparency and Explainability: AI decision-making processes should be understandable and interpretable by humans.

7. Privacy and Data Protection: AI systems must safeguard user information and respect privacy rights.

8. Accountability: Clear lines of responsibility must be established for AI decisions and their consequences.

9. Safety and Security: Robust measures should be in place to prevent unintended consequences and protect against malicious exploitation.

10. Human Rights and Dignity: AI systems must respect human rights, democratic values, and individual autonomy.

11. Beneficial Outcomes: AI should be developed to augment human capabilities, advance inclusion, and protect the environment.

The Importance of Ethics in Machine Learning and Decision-Making Systems

Ethics in AI is crucial for several reasons:

1. Mitigating Risks: Ethical frameworks help prevent bias, ensure privacy, and mitigate potential harms.

2. Building Trust: Transparent and accountable AI systems foster public confidence in the technology.

3. Societal Impact: AI has broad implications for society, with the potential for both positive and negative effects.

4. Legal Compliance: Ethical AI practices often align with emerging regulations and data protection laws.

5. Sustainable Innovation: Balancing innovation with ethical considerations ensures responsible AI development.

Historical Context and Evolution of AI Ethics

The field of AI ethics has evolved significantly:

1. Early Concerns: Initial ethical discussions in AI focused on safety and control of intelligent systems.

2. Emergence of Frameworks: As AI became more prevalent, organizations began developing ethical guidelines. The IEEE's Ethically Aligned Design and the EU's Ethics Guidelines for Trustworthy AI are notable examples.

3. International Standards: The OECD AI Principles, adopted in May 2019, became the first intergovernmental standard on AI.

4. Ongoing Development: AI ethics continues to evolve, with increasing focus on issues like algorithmic bias, privacy in machine learning, and the societal impacts of AI deployment.

5. Integration into Development: There's a growing emphasis on embedding ethical considerations into the earliest stages of AI system design, rather than addressing them post-deployment.

As AI technology advances, the field of AI ethics remains dynamic, adapting to new challenges and societal expectations. The focus has shifted from theoretical concerns to practical implementation of ethical principles throughout the AI lifecycle.

Bias in AI Systems

Bias in AI systems is a critical issue that can lead to unfair and discriminatory outcomes. Here's a detailed look at the types, sources, impacts, and mitigation strategies for AI bias:

Types of Bias in Machine Learning Algorithms

1. Historical Bias: Reflects past prejudices present in historical data.

2. Sample Bias: Occurs when training data isn't representative of the population.

3. Label Bias: Results from inconsistent or subjective data labeling.

4. Aggregation Bias: Arises when data is combined inappropriately, obscuring important distinctions.

5. Confirmation Bias: The tendency to favor information confirming existing beliefs.

6. Evaluation Bias: Emerges when the model is tested on a limited or non-representative dataset.

Sources of Bias: Data, Algorithms, and Human Factors

1. Data Bias:

    - Incomplete or skewed training datasets.

    - Measurement bias due to inaccurate data collection methods.

    - Exclusion or reporting bias when important data points are omitted.

2. Algorithmic Bias:

    - Flaws in the algorithm's design or parameters.

    - Automation bias, where automated results are preferred over human judgment.

3. Human Factors:

- Cognitive biases of developers influencing model design.
- Prejudice bias reflecting societal stereotypes.
- Selection bias in choosing training data.

Impact of Biased AI on Different Demographics and Society

Biased AI systems can have far-reaching consequences:

- Perpetuation of societal biases and stereotypes.
- Unfair treatment in job recruitment, potentially excluding qualified applicants.
- Discriminatory outcomes in healthcare, finance, and criminal justice systems.
- Reinforcement of gender, racial, and socioeconomic inequalities.

Strategies for Detecting and Mitigating Bias

1. Bias Detection:

   - Implement bias detection algorithms and audits.
   - Use metrics to measure fairness and bias in model outputs.
   - Regularly monitor AI systems post-deployment.

2. Data Preprocessing:

   - Collect diverse and representative datasets.
   - Apply techniques like resampling and reweighting to balance data.

3. Algorithmic Adjustments:
    - Implement fairness constraints in model design.
    - Use adversarial debiasing techniques.
4. Transparency and Explainability:
    - Enhance model interpretability to identify sources of bias.
    - Provide explanations for model decisions.
5. Diverse Development Teams:
    - Foster interdisciplinary collaboration to bring varied perspectives.
6. Continuous Evaluation:
    - Establish ongoing monitoring and evaluation processes.
    - Conduct regular bias audits and impact assessments.

By implementing these strategies, organizations can work towards developing more fair and equitable AI systems that benefit society as a whole.

Fairness and Transparency in AI

Fairness and transparency are crucial aspects of ethical AI systems. Let's explore these concepts in detail:

Defining Fairness in the Context of AI Systems

Fairness in AI refers to ensuring that machine learning models treat all individuals and groups equitably. However, defining fairness is complex and context-dependent. There are three key perspectives on fairness in AI:

1. Equality: Treating everyone the same, regardless of background.

2. Equity: Recognizing different needs and providing extra support where necessary.

3. Justice: Ensuring fair AI development processes and equitable distribution of outcomes.

Fairness metrics help measure and reduce bias in AI models. They allow developers to identify unfair treatment of certain groups, evaluate model performance against fairness goals, and guide model development to avoid bias1.

Transparency and Explainability in AI Decision-Making

AI transparency refers to the openness and clarity about how AI systems work, make decisions, and learn over time. Transparent AI systems allow stakeholders to understand the logic behind AI-generated outcomes, fostering trust and accountability.

Explainable AI (XAI) is a key component of transparency. It involves developing AI systems that can explain their decisions in a manner understandable to humans. This helps stakeholders interpret and justify AI decisions, ensuring that there are no hidden mechanisms or biases.

Trade-offs Between Model Performance and Interpretability

There is often a tension between model performance and interpretability. More complex models may achieve higher accuracy but be less transparent. Balancing these factors is crucial:

- Highly accurate models may still be unfair or opaque.

- Simpler, more interpretable models might sacrifice some performance.

- Regular fairness metric checks during training and testing help refine models to balance performance with fairness.

Tools and Techniques for Enhancing AI Transparency

Several approaches can enhance AI transparency:

1. Open-Source Code and Models: Sharing AI system source code and model details allows for independent review and validation.

2. Model Auditing: Regular audits by internal or external experts ensure compliance with ethical standards and identify potential biases.

3. Data Provenance Documentation: Maintaining detailed records of training data sources and processing methods ensures data accuracy and representativeness.

4. Interpretability Methods: Techniques that provide insights into model behavior and decision-making processes.

5. AI Assurance Frameworks: Guidelines like those provided by digital.gov.au offer steps for ensuring fairness in AI systems.

By implementing these tools and techniques, organizations can develop more transparent, fair, and trustworthy AI systems that balance performance with ethical considerations.

Privacy and Data Protection

Privacy and data protection are critical concerns in the age of AI. Here's a detailed look at key aspects:

AI's Impact on Personal Privacy

AI technologies have significant implications for personal privacy:

- Vast data collection: AI systems often rely on large amounts of personal data, including sensitive information like medical records and financial details.

- Surveillance capabilities: AI-powered facial recognition and monitoring systems raise concerns about privacy in public spaces.

- Predictive analytics: AI can make predictions about individuals' behaviors and preferences, potentially infringing on privacy.

Data Protection Regulations and Their Implications for AI

Several regulations aim to protect personal data in AI systems:

- GDPR: Requires AI systems to comply with principles like purpose limitation and data minimization.

- Preventive assessments: High-risk AI applications may require preventive data protection assessments.

- Right to explanation: Individuals may have the right to explanations of automated decisions affecting them.

Ethical Considerations in Data Collection and Usage

Key ethical principles for AI data collection and usage include:

- Consent: Obtaining informed, freely given, and revocable permission from individuals.

- Fairness: Ensuring data use doesn't perpetuate biases or cause harm.

- Intention: Using data for purposes that serve societal interests.

- Integrity: Maintaining accuracy and reliability of collected data.
- Stewardship: Protecting data in a secure environment.

Privacy-Preserving Machine Learning Techniques

Several techniques aim to protect privacy in AI systems:

- Differential Privacy: Adds controlled noise to data to prevent re-identification.
- Federated Learning: Allows model training on decentralized data without sharing raw information.
- Homomorphic Encryption: Enables computations on encrypted data without decryption.
- Secure Multi-Party Computation: Allows multiple parties to jointly compute functions without revealing inputs.

Privacy-preserving frameworks like TensorFlow Privacy, OpenMined, and PySyft implement these techniques to enable secure and private machine learning.

By adopting these privacy-preserving approaches and adhering to ethical principles, organizations can harness the power of AI while protecting individual privacy and complying with regulations.

Accountability and Responsibility in AI Systems

Accountability and responsibility in AI systems are crucial for ensuring ethical and responsible use of artificial intelligence. Here's a detailed look at key aspects:

Challenges in Assigning Responsibility for AI Decisions

Assigning responsibility for AI decisions is complex due to several factors:

- Opacity of AI systems: The "black box" nature of many AI algorithms makes it difficult to trace decision-making processes.
- Multiple stakeholders: AI systems often involve numerous parties, including developers, users, and deployers, complicating responsibility attribution.
- Autonomous decision-making: As AI systems become more autonomous, traditional accountability models face challenges5.

Legal and Ethical Frameworks for AI Accountability

Several frameworks are emerging to address AI accountability:

- Regulatory compliance: Laws like GDPR and CCPA require organizations to ensure AI systems comply with data protection regulations.
- Ethical guidelines: The IEEE Global Initiative on Ethics of Autonomous and Intelligent Systems provides principles for ethical AI development.
- AI-specific regulations: The EU's Artificial Intelligence Act proposes comprehensive rules for high-risk AI systems.

The Role of Human Oversight in AI Systems

Human oversight is essential for responsible AI use:

- Design considerations: AI systems should be designed to enable effective human oversight throughout their lifecycle.
- Intervention capabilities: Humans must be able to intervene, override, or halt AI systems when necessary.

- Awareness of limitations: Overseers should understand AI system capabilities and limitations to prevent over-reliance.

Auditing and Monitoring AI for Responsible Use

Regular auditing and monitoring are crucial for maintaining AI accountability:

- Data auditing: Examining the accuracy, completeness, and potential biases in AI training data.
- Algorithm auditing: Reviewing AI algorithms for potential biases, errors, or unintended consequences.
- Outcome auditing: Evaluating AI-generated results for fairness and consistency with expected outcomes.
- Continuous improvement: Implementing ongoing monitoring and evaluation processes to detect and address issues promptly.

By addressing these aspects of accountability and responsibility, organizations can work towards developing and deploying AI systems that are not only powerful but also ethical and trustworthy.

AI and Social Impact

AI systems have profound implications for society, offering both significant benefits and potential risks. Here's a detailed look at AI's social impact:

Potential Societal Benefits and Risks of AI Systems

Benefits:

- Improved process efficiency and productivity

- Enhanced creativity by automating repetitive tasks
- Lower risk of errors in critical sectors like healthcare
- Assistance in dangerous tasks, improving human safety
- Addressing complex global challenges like climate change

Risks:

- Opacity in decision-making processes
- Potential for bias and discrimination
- Threats to privacy and fundamental rights
- Safety concerns, especially in critical sectors
- Social manipulation and spread of misinformation

AI's Influence on Employment and Economic Structures

- Job displacement: AI automation may lead to significant job losses, particularly affecting low-skilled workers
- Economic inequality: AI could exacerbate wealth disparities by disproportionately benefiting wealthy individuals and corporations
- Shift in job market: While some jobs may be lost, new roles related to AI development and maintenance may emerge
- Productivity gains: AI can boost productivity, potentially leading to economic growth

Ethical Considerations in AI-Driven Automation

- Corporate accountability: Companies deploying AI have a responsibility to consider the broader impact of job displacement

- Fair distribution of benefits: Ethical imperative to ensure AI-driven productivity gains are distributed equitably

- Transparency and explainability: AI systems should be auditable and traceable to ensure ethical deployment

- Human-centric approach: Emphasis on empowering human agents and maintaining human oversight in AI systems

Ensuring Equitable Access to AI Technologies

- Addressing the digital divide: Ensuring AI benefits are accessible across different socioeconomic groups

- Education and reskilling: Implementing programs to help workers adapt to AI-driven changes in the job market

- Inclusive development: Fostering collaboration between AI developers, data scientists, and domain experts to ensure ethical decision-making

- Regulatory frameworks: Developing policies to govern AI development and deployment, promoting responsible and equitable use

By addressing these aspects, we can work towards harnessing the benefits of AI while mitigating its potential negative impacts on society.

Ethical AI Design and Development

Ethical AI design and development is crucial for creating responsible and beneficial artificial intelligence systems. Here's a detailed look at key aspects:

Incorporating Ethics into the AI Development Lifecycle

Ethical considerations should be integrated throughout the AI development process:

- Problem Definition: Clearly define ethical goals and potential impacts from the outset.
- Data Collection and Preparation: Ensure diverse, representative datasets and address potential biases.
- Model Selection and Training: Prioritize explainability and fairness in algorithm design.
- Validation and Testing: Implement rigorous testing for bias and ethical concerns.
- Deployment: Establish human oversight mechanisms and clear boundaries for AI decision-making.
- Monitoring and Maintenance: Continuously audit for ethical issues and performance drift.

Ethical Guidelines and Best Practices for AI Practitioners

AI practitioners should adhere to established ethical principles:

- Transparency and Explainability: Ensure AI systems are interpretable and their decision-making processes can be understood.

- Fairness and Non-discrimination: Actively work to identify and mitigate biases in AI systems.
- Privacy and Data Protection: Implement robust measures to safeguard user information.
- Accountability: Establish clear lines of responsibility for AI decisions and outcomes.
- Human-Centered Values: Prioritize human well-being and societal benefit in AI development.

The Role of Diverse Teams in Creating Ethical AI

Diverse teams are essential for developing ethical AI systems:

- Representation: Include team members from various backgrounds, genders, races, and disciplines.
- Multidisciplinary Expertise: Involve experts from fields such as ethics, social sciences, and law alongside technical specialists.
- Improved Problem-Solving: Diverse teams are better equipped to identify and address potential ethical issues.
- Innovation: Diversity drives creative thinking and leads to more ethical and inclusive AI solutions.

Case Studies of Ethical AI Implementation

Several organizations have implemented ethical AI practices:

- Google: Published a 2022 Diversity Annual Report detailing actions taken to build an inclusive workplace.
- Microsoft: Integrated diversity and inclusion principles into hiring, communication, and product development.

- OpenAI: Implemented red-teaming strategies for ChatGPT, collaborating with various experts to identify and address potential ethical concerns.

By incorporating these ethical considerations, guidelines, and diverse perspectives, organizations can develop AI systems that are not only powerful but also responsible and beneficial to society.

Future Challenges and Opportunities in AI Ethics

Emerging Ethical Issues in Advanced AI Systems

As AI systems become more sophisticated, new ethical challenges are emerging:

- Autonomous decision-making: Advanced AI systems may make critical decisions without human oversight, raising questions about accountability and control.

- Deepfakes and misinformation: AI-generated content poses risks to truth and trust in society.

- Algorithmic bias: As AI systems become more complex, detecting and mitigating biases becomes increasingly challenging.

- Privacy concerns: The ability of AI to process vast amounts of personal data raises concerns about data protection and individual privacy.

The Potential for AI in Addressing Global Challenges

AI offers significant opportunities to tackle pressing global issues:

- Climate change: AI can analyze climate data, predict weather patterns, and optimize resource usage to combat climate change.

- Healthcare: AI-powered systems can improve disease diagnosis, treatment planning, and drug discovery.

- Poverty and inequality: AI can help optimize resource allocation and identify effective interventions to reduce poverty.

Balancing Innovation with Ethical Considerations

Striking a balance between AI innovation and ethics is crucial:

- Ethical guidelines: Developing comprehensive ethical frameworks for AI development and deployment.

- Transparency and explainability: Ensuring AI systems are interpretable and their decision-making processes can be understood.

- Diverse teams: Including experts from various disciplines to identify and address potential ethical issues.

The Role of Policy and Governance in Shaping Ethical AI

Policy and governance play a critical role in ensuring ethical AI development:

- Regulatory frameworks: Developing adaptive regulations that promote innovation while safeguarding ethical standards.

- International cooperation: Fostering global collaboration to address AI ethics challenges that transcend national boundaries.

- Education and awareness: Promoting AI ethics education to ensure developers and users understand the ethical implications of AI systems.

By addressing these future challenges and opportunities, we can work towards developing AI systems that are not only powerful and innovative but also ethical and beneficial to society.

In conclusion, the ethical landscape of artificial intelligence is both complex and dynamic, presenting a myriad of challenges and opportunities as we navigate the future of this transformative technology. As AI continues to evolve, it is imperative that we prioritize ethical considerations at every stage of development and deployment. By fostering transparency, accountability, and inclusivity, we can harness the potential of AI to address pressing global issues while safeguarding fundamental human rights and values. The collaborative efforts of policymakers, technologists, ethicists, and diverse stakeholders will be essential in shaping a future where AI serves as a force for good. As we move forward, let us remain vigilant in our commitment to ethical AI practices, ensuring that the innovations we create not only enhance our capabilities but also enrich our society as a whole.

Chapter 6: Future of Human-AI Communication

As we stand on the brink of a new era in technology, the way we communicate with artificial intelligence is poised for a profound transformation. The evolution of human-AI communication promises to redefine our interactions, making them more natural, intuitive, and seamless. With advancements in natural language processing, machine learning, and multimodal interfaces, the potential for AI systems to understand and respond to human emotions, intentions, and nuances is becoming increasingly feasible.

In this chapter, we will explore the exciting developments in AI-powered virtual assistants and chatbots that are reshaping our daily lives. These intelligent systems are not only enhancing productivity but also personalizing our experiences across various domains, from healthcare to customer service. As we delve deeper into the future of work, we will examine how AI is transforming collaboration between humans and machines, fostering a new paradigm where augmented intelligence enhances human capabilities rather than replacing them.

Furthermore, we will consider the ethical implications of these advancements and the societal changes they may bring. As AI becomes an integral part of our communication landscape, understanding its impact on our relationships, creativity, and workplace dynamics is essential. Join us as we navigate the promising yet complex future of human-AI communication, where technology and humanity converge to create new possibilities for connection and collaboration.

Evolution of Human-AI Interfaces

The evolution of human-AI interfaces is rapidly transforming how we interact with technology, moving towards more intuitive and seamless communication methods.

Natural Language Processing Advancements

Natural Language Processing (NLP) has seen significant progress in recent years:

- Large language models like GPT-3 have revolutionized AI's ability to understand and generate human-like text.

- These models can now perform complex tasks such as programming, solving math problems, and engaging in high-level conversations.

- NLP is enabling more natural interactions with AI assistants, improving tasks like sentiment analysis, language translation, and text summarization.

Multimodal Interaction: Voice, Gesture, and Visual Interfaces

The future of human-AI interaction is becoming increasingly multimodal:

- Voice-activated virtual assistants like Siri and Alexa demonstrate the growing capabilities of voice interfaces.

- Hybrid interaction interfaces are emerging, combining traditional graphical user interfaces (GUIs) with AI-powered intent-based interaction.

- Visual interfaces are advancing, with AI models like DALL·E 2 capable of generating images from text descriptions.

Brain-Computer Interfaces and Direct Neural Communication

Brain-Computer Interfaces (BCIs) represent the cutting edge of human-AI interaction:

- BCIs create a direct communication pathway between the brain's electrical activity and external devices.
- These interfaces can capture electrophysiological signals from neurons and translate them into actions.
- BCIs range from non-invasive (EEG) to invasive (microelectrode arrays) methods, with varying degrees of signal clarity.
- Research in BCIs has shown promise in assisting individuals with neuromuscular disorders to communicate and control devices.

As these technologies continue to advance, we can expect more intuitive, personalized, and immersive interactions between humans and AI systems, potentially redefining our relationship with technology.

AI-Powered Virtual Assistants and Chatbots

AI-powered virtual assistants and chatbots are rapidly evolving, offering increasingly sophisticated and personalized interactions across various domains.

Personalization and Context-Awareness in AI Assistants

AI assistants are becoming more adept at understanding and adapting to user contexts:

- Advanced machine learning algorithms process user preferences, historical interactions, and behavioral patterns to anticipate needs and deliver relevant responses.

- Context-aware systems analyze environmental signals like location data and time-sensitive information to create highly personalized experiences.
- These assistants maintain conversational context across multiple interactions, eliminating the need for users to repeat information.

Emotional Intelligence and Empathy in AI Communication

Empathetic AI is revolutionizing human-machine interaction:

- AI systems are being trained to recognize emotions through facial recognition, speech patterns, and text analysis.
- Sentiment analysis capabilities allow chatbots to detect emotions in customer messages and tailor their responses accordingly.
- By 2024, 71% of customers believe AI will make customer experiences more empathetic.

Integration of AI Assistants in Various Domains

Healthcare

- Virtual Health Assistants (VHAs) are transforming patient support by handling tasks like scheduling appointments and managing patient data entries.
- AI-powered health assistants can track vital signs and patient behavior patterns to provide proactive care recommendations.
- These systems streamline appointment scheduling by considering factors like patient location and mobility status.

Education

- AI assistants in education deliver personalized learning experiences by adapting content difficulty and teaching styles based on student performance and learning patterns.

- Customer Service
- AI-powered chatbots dramatically improve response accuracy and resolution times in customer support operations.

- These systems can handle multiple customer inquiries simultaneously while maintaining personalization based on purchase history and previous support interactions.

As AI technology continues to advance, we can expect even more sophisticated and empathetic virtual assistants integrated across various sectors, enhancing user experiences and improving efficiency.

Augmented Intelligence and Human-AI Collaboration

Augmented Intelligence and Human-AI Collaboration are transforming the way humans and machines work together, enhancing our cognitive abilities and problem-solving capabilities.

AI as a Cognitive Enhancement Tool

Augmented intelligence focuses on using AI to enhance human abilities rather than replace them:

- AI systems analyze vast amounts of data to provide insights and recommendations, empowering humans to make better-informed decisions.

- This approach amplifies human intelligence, fostering greater innovation, productivity, and strategic thinking.

- AI supports human creativity by handling data-heavy tasks, allowing humans to focus on higher-level cognitive functions.

Collaborative Problem-Solving Between Humans and AI

Human-AI collaboration leverages the strengths of both parties:

- AI excels at processing information, detecting patterns, and making predictions, while humans excel in creativity, problem-solving, and strategic decision-making.

- In marketing, AI analyzes customer data to spot trends, while human marketers use these insights to create impactful campaigns.

- This collaborative approach leads to more effective and innovative outcomes across various industries.

Ethical Considerations in Human-AI Partnerships

As human-AI collaboration becomes more prevalent, several ethical considerations emerge:

- Ensuring fairness in AI decision-making and protecting privacy rights are crucial aspects of responsible human-AI collaboration.

- Transparency in AI processes and establishing clear accountability frameworks are essential for building trust.

- Only 35% of global consumers currently trust how organizations implement AI technology, highlighting the need for enhanced transparency and accountability.

- Ethical design principles must be prioritized to prevent unintended and potentially harmful consequences of AI-driven decisions.

By addressing these ethical considerations and fostering a collaborative approach, we can harness the full potential of human-AI partnerships while maintaining human agency and ethical integrity in an increasingly AI-augmented world.

AI in Social Interactions and Relationships

AI Companions and Social Robots

AI companions and social robots are becoming increasingly sophisticated:

- Companion robots like ElliQ engage in simple interactions, providing companionship over activities like having tea or coffee.
- More advanced AI companions like Replika offer personalized emotional support through text conversations.
- Holographic AI companions like Gatebox's avatar can manage smart home devices and create a sense of presence for those living alone.
- Humanoid robots like Harmony by RealDoll aim to provide romantic and physical connections.

Impact of AI on Human Social Skills and Relationships

The growing presence of AI in social interactions is having significant effects:

- AI companions may help combat loneliness, especially among socially isolated older adults.
- There are concerns that relying on AI for companionship could lead to increased social isolation.
- Some individuals may prefer AI relationships due to their predictability and customization.
- AI companions like Matilda can help people stay connected with loved ones and caregivers through video calls and messaging.

Ethical Implications of Emotional Bonds with AI Entities

The development of emotional connections with AI raises several ethical concerns:

- There are worries about the long-term psychological effects of forming attachments to entities lacking genuine emotions or consciousness.
- The use of AI companions challenges conventional ideas of companionship, love, and emotional bonds.
- Ethical guidelines are needed to ensure AI companions are designed responsibly, with transparency and safeguards for vulnerable individuals.
- Research suggests that machines may be held to higher moral standards than humans in social interactions.

As AI companions become more prevalent, it is crucial to balance their potential benefits with careful consideration of their impact on human relationships and social skills. Ongoing research and ethical frameworks will be essential in navigating this new frontier of human-AI interaction.

Language Translation and Cross-Cultural Communication

Real-time Language Translation and Interpretation

Real-time translation technology has advanced significantly, enabling instant communication across language barriers:

- AI-powered tools like Google Translate, Microsoft Translator, and Smartling Translate can now translate text and speech in real-time across hundreds of languages.

- These systems use neural machine translation (NMT) to understand context and patterns, producing more natural translations.

- Real-time translation is accessible through smartphones and computers, making global communication possible for anyone.

- Google Translate supports 109 languages and translates over 100 billion words daily, while Microsoft Translator covers over 60 languages.

AI-powered Cultural Context Understanding

While AI has made strides in translation, understanding cultural nuances remains challenging:

- AI systems trained on internet data may perpetuate cultural biases or misunderstandings.

- Current AI models struggle with concepts like sarcasm, humor, and cultural taboos that vary across cultures.

- Experiments with advanced AI like Google Gemini Advanced show slight improvements in cultural understanding, but genuine cultural fluency remains elusive.

- AI representations of cultural context often prioritize commercial interests and popular tourist attractions over diverse local experiences.

Bridging Communication Gaps in Global Interactions

AI is playing an increasing role in facilitating cross-cultural communication:

- Real-time translation significantly reduces language barriers in various settings, from business meetings to travel.

- AI can augment our understanding of urban spaces and cultural contexts, potentially enhancing social cohesion and diversity.

- However, AI's current limitations in grasping cultural nuances mean human expertise remains crucial for sensitive cross-cultural interactions.

- Future developments aim to create AI systems that can adapt to individual cultural backgrounds in real-time, enhancing global understanding and cultural empathy.

As AI technology continues to evolve, it holds great potential for bridging communication gaps. However, it's crucial to approach these advancements thoughtfully, ensuring AI enhances rather than diminishes the richness of human cultural exchange.

AI in Creative Expression and Art

AI as a Tool for Artistic Creation and Collaboration

AI has become a powerful collaborator in the creative process across various artistic disciplines:

- Visual artists use AI image generators like DALL-E 2 and Midjourney to visualize complex scenes and explore new artistic directions.

- Musicians leverage AI algorithms to generate initial compositions and explore new melodic possibilities.

- Interior designers use specialized AI tools to rapidly generate multiple design concepts for client presentations.

- In advertising, creative teams use AI to generate initial concepts and visualizations.

- AI serves as a sophisticated sketching partner, generating initial ideas that artists can refine and develop. This collaboration enhances creative output by allowing artists to explore a wider array of concepts and iterations swiftly.

Generative AI in Music, Visual Arts, and Literature

Generative AI is transforming various creative fields:

- In visual arts, Generative Adversarial Networks (GANs) create realistic and abstract artworks.

- AI algorithms in music can analyze existing pieces and generate original melodies in various styles.

- ACE Studio demonstrates how AI can deploy AI vocalists on top of music tracks.

- In literature, AI-generated poetry, storytelling, and editorial aid have transformed the writing process, helping authors overcome creative obstacles.

- Generative AI acts as a "probabilities paintbrush," using millions of probabilistic functions to produce outcomes based on learned patterns6. This approach allows for new forms of artistic expression and democratizes art creation.

Implications for Copyright and Authorship

The integration of AI in creative processes raises several ethical and legal concerns:

- Questions of authorship arise when AI is involved in creating artworks, compositions, or written pieces.

- Copyright issues emerge regarding AI-generated work and appropriate compensation for original authors whose work may have inspired AI results.
- The ability of AI to produce potentially deceptive or plagiarized content threatens the integrity of creative fields.
- These challenges require deliberate analysis and the development of legislative frameworks to ensure responsible use of AI in creative industries. The blurring of lines between human and machine creativity necessitates a reevaluation of traditional concepts of authorship and originality.

As AI continues to evolve, its role in artistic creation promises to be increasingly integral and transformative. However, it's crucial to maintain a balance that fosters genuine creativity rather than dilutes individual expression

Future Workplace Dynamics

AI-augmented Work Environments

AI is transforming workplace environments, creating more connected and efficient spaces:

- By 2025, 72% of organizations are expected to have adopted some form of AI, up from around 50% in previous years.
- AI-powered IoT integrations enable smart workplaces that automatically adjust lighting, HVAC, and other building systems based on occupancy and usage patterns, leading to energy savings and improved employee comfort.

- AI algorithms analyze workplace occupancy and utilization data to optimize space use, predicting future requirements and informing decisions about office layouts and hybrid work models.

Reskilling and Adapting to AI-integrated Workplaces

The integration of AI necessitates significant workforce reskilling:

- 90% of jobs are likely to be significantly impacted by generative AI in the coming decade.

- Executives estimate about 40% of their workforce needs to reskill over the next 3 years.

- Organizations are focusing on both reskilling their existing workforce and tapping into additional talent pools to prepare for the AI-driven future.

- Companies are providing guidelines on responsible AI use to help employees harness its benefits while ensuring ethical, secure, and compliant applications.

Balancing Automation and Human Expertise

Finding the right balance between AI automation and human expertise is crucial:

- AI should be used as a tool, with humans maintaining oversight and strategic input.

- Humans should focus on strategic and creative tasks, while AI handles routine or data-intensive work.

- The World Economic Forum predicts that new technologies will disrupt 85 million jobs globally between 2020 and 2025, but also create 97 million new job roles.

- Organizations need to clearly define roles and responsibilities for AI and human experts, establish guidelines for AI use, and provide training for professionals on effective AI tool utilization.

By embracing these dynamics, organizations can create more efficient, adaptive, and innovative workplaces that leverage the strengths of both AI and human expertise.

Ethical and Societal Implications

Privacy Concerns in Advanced Human-AI Communication

As AI communication technologies become more sophisticated, privacy concerns are intensifying:

- AI systems often rely on vast amounts of personal data, including sensitive information like medical records and financial details, raising concerns about data security and unauthorized access.

- The collection and processing of personal data by AI systems increase the risk of data breaches, potentially exposing individuals to identity theft and other privacy violations.

- AI-powered surveillance technologies, particularly in law enforcement, are sparking debates about the balance between security and personal freedoms.

- Generative AI models trained on public data may inadvertently include personal information collected without individuals' knowledge or consent, making it difficult for people to control their data.

Transparency and Trust in AI-Human Interactions

Transparency and trust are crucial yet complex aspects of AI-human interactions:

- Explainable AI (XAI) aims to make AI decision-making processes more transparent, but there's a tension between explainability and genuine trust.

- The complexity of AI systems often makes it challenging for organizations to explain how personal information is used and how AI-driven decisions are made.

- Human-centered explanations in AI systems can increase reliance on AI recommendations, but the effect varies depending on the decision-making context.

- As of 2025, only 35% of global consumers trust how organizations implement AI technology, highlighting the need for enhanced transparency and accountability.

Societal Impact of Widespread AI Communication Technologies

The proliferation of AI communication technologies is having far-reaching societal effects:

- AI assistants and chatbots are transforming various sectors, including healthcare, education, and customer service, potentially improving efficiency but also raising concerns about job displacement.

- The integration of AI in creative fields is challenging traditional notions of authorship and copyright, necessitating new legal frameworks.

- AI-powered language translation and cross-cultural communication tools are breaking down language barriers but may struggle with cultural nuances and context.

- There are growing concerns about AI's potential to exacerbate existing societal biases and inequalities, particularly in areas like hiring, lending, and criminal justice.

As AI communication technologies continue to advance, it is crucial to address these ethical and societal implications proactively. This includes developing robust privacy protections, enhancing AI transparency, fostering public trust, and ensuring equitable access to AI benefits across society.

As we conclude our exploration of the future of human-AI communication, it is clear that we stand at a pivotal moment in technological history. The rapid advancements in AI are reshaping our society in profound ways, offering immense potential for progress while simultaneously presenting complex ethical challenges.

The integration of AI into our daily lives and workplaces promises enhanced efficiency, improved decision-making, and innovative solutions to global problems. However, we must remain vigilant in addressing the ethical implications of these technologies, particularly in areas of privacy, transparency, and fairness. As AI systems become more sophisticated, it is crucial that we maintain human oversight and ensure that these technologies augment rather than replace human capabilities.

Looking ahead, the success of human-AI collaboration will depend on our ability to strike a delicate balance between innovation and ethical considerations. By fostering responsible AI development, prioritizing human wellbeing, and promoting inclusivity, we can harness the transformative power of AI to create a future that benefits all of humanity.

As we navigate this AI-driven future, it is imperative that we continue to engage in thoughtful dialogue, develop robust ethical frameworks, and remain adaptable to the evolving landscape of human-AI interaction. By doing so, we can work towards a future where artificial intelligence enhances our lives, empowers our creativity, and upholds our shared values as a society.

Conclusion: Bridging Two Worlds

As we stand at the forefront of a new era in human-AI communication, it is clear that the synergy between human intelligence and artificial intelligence is reshaping our world in profound ways. The rapid advancements in AI technologies are not just transforming how we interact with machines, but are fundamentally altering the landscape of human communication itself.

This final chapter aims to synthesize the key insights we've explored throughout this book, emphasizing the critical importance of understanding and harnessing the potential of AI communication. As we've seen, AI is no longer just a tool for automation or data processing; it has become an active participant in our communicative processes, capable of generating content, facilitating cross-cultural understanding, and even engaging in creative endeavors.

However, as we embrace these technological advancements, we must also grapple with the ethical implications and societal impacts they bring. The future of human-AI collaboration holds immense promise, but it also requires us to carefully consider how we can maintain human agency, creativity, and ethical judgment in an increasingly AI-integrated world.

Key Insights on AI Communication

Recap of Major Developments in Human-AI Interfaces

Human-AI interfaces have evolved significantly over the years:

- The progression from command-line interfaces to graphical user interfaces (GUIs) and touchscreens has made technology more accessible to the general public.

- Voice-activated virtual assistants like Siri, Alexa, and Google Assistant have revolutionized how we interact with AI, allowing for natural language communication.

- Extended Reality (XR) technologies are emerging as new testbeds for human-AI interactions, offering rapid prototyping and systematic investigation of these interactions.

- Brain-Computer Interfaces (BCIs) represent the cutting edge of human-AI interaction, creating direct communication pathways between the brain and external devices.

Evolution of AI Assistants and Chatbots

AI assistants and chatbots have come a long way since their inception:

- ELIZA, created in the 1960s, was one of the first chatbots, using simple pattern-matching techniques to simulate conversation.

- Advancements in Natural Language Processing (NLP) have enabled modern chatbots to understand context, user intent, and respond more naturally.

- Recent developments like GPT-3 have raised the bar for AI-driven conversational agents, offering more sophisticated and human-like interactions.

- AI assistants are now integrated into various aspects of daily life, from smart homes to navigation systems, offering personalized and adaptive experiences.

Importance of Ethical Considerations in AI Development

As AI becomes more prevalent, ethical considerations are paramount:

- Bias and fairness are major concerns, as AI systems can perpetuate and amplify biases present in their training data.

- Transparency in AI decision-making is crucial for accountability and building trust with users.
- Privacy and data protection are significant challenges, especially as AI systems process vast amounts of personal information.
- Continuous evaluation and auditing of AI systems for ethical considerations are necessary to ensure responsible development and deployment.
- Ethical AI design requires multidisciplinary collaboration, including ethicists, policymakers, and end-users.

By addressing these ethical considerations and continuing to advance human-AI interfaces and AI assistants, we can work towards creating AI systems that are not only powerful but also trustworthy and beneficial to society.

The Synergy of Human and Artificial Intelligence

AI as an Amplifier of Human Cognitive Abilities

AI has emerged as a powerful tool to enhance human cognitive capabilities, enabling individuals and organizations to process vast amounts of information and solve complex problems more efficiently:

- Data Processing and Decision-Making: AI systems excel at analyzing extensive datasets, identifying patterns, and providing actionable insights. For instance, in healthcare, AI-powered diagnostic tools assist doctors in detecting diseases with higher accuracy, while in finance, AI helps analysts predict market trends for better investment decisions.

- Creativity Enhancement: AI tools like Autodesk's Dreamcatcher generate thousands of potential designs based on user-defined criteria, sparking new ideas and allowing designers to focus on aesthetic and professional judgment6. Similarly, generative AI models aid writers, artists, and musicians in exploring creative possibilities beyond human limitations.

- Cognitive Load Management: By offloading routine or data-intensive tasks to AI systems, humans can conserve mental energy for strategic thinking and innovation. This partnership optimizes cognitive load management, allowing individuals to focus on higher-order skills like critical analysis and problem-solving.

Balancing Automation with Human Expertise

The integration of AI into various industries necessitates a careful balance between automation and human oversight:

- Complementary Strengths: While AI excels at precision, efficiency, and repetitive tasks, humans bring creativity, intuition, and ethical judgment to the table. For example, in manufacturing, AI optimizes processes like cutting speeds and material usage, but skilled engineers are still required to oversee complex designs and ensure quality standards are met.

- Guidelines for Collaboration: Organizations must clearly define roles for humans and AI to ensure effective collaboration. This includes training professionals to use AI tools effectively while incorporating human oversight at critical decision points.

- New Job Roles: As AI automates routine tasks, new opportunities are emerging in areas like AI management and optimization. This shift highlights the importance of continuous learning and reskilling to adapt to evolving workplace dynamics.

The Role of Emotional Intelligence in the AI Era

Emotional intelligence (EI) is becoming increasingly vital as humans collaborate with AI systems:

- Fostering Empathy: While AI excels at logical reasoning and data analysis, it lacks the ability to understand or respond to human emotions. Emotional intelligence bridges this gap by enabling humans to interpret emotional contexts in interactions with both other humans and AI systems.

- Ethical Decision-Making: EI plays a crucial role in ensuring that decisions made with the assistance of AI align with human values and societal welfare. It helps individuals recognize potential biases or limitations in AI systems, promoting transparency and accountability.

- Human-AI Collaboration: Incorporating emotional intelligence into the design of AI systems allows them to respond empathetically to human needs. This leads to more personalized experiences while fostering harmonious collaboration between humans and machines.

By leveraging the strengths of both human intelligence and artificial intelligence, we can create a synergistic relationship that amplifies productivity, enhances creativity, and ensures ethical outcomes. This partnership exemplifies how technology can empower humanity rather than replace it.

Shaping a Connected Future

AI's Potential to Address Global Challenges

AI has emerged as a powerful tool for tackling some of humanity's most pressing issues:

- Climate Change: AI can analyze vast amounts of climate data, weather patterns, and historical records to identify trends and provide insights into mitigation strategies. For instance, AI-powered tools can track ecosystems by processing large quantities of data from satellite imagery and drone footage.

- Healthcare: AI is revolutionizing healthcare diagnoses and treatment approaches. AI-powered diagnostic tools assist doctors in detecting diseases with higher accuracy.

- Poverty and Inequality: AI can help optimize resource allocation and identify effective interventions to reduce poverty. It also has the potential to improve food production and resource efficiency through AI-driven automation in agriculture.

The Importance of Responsible AI Development

As AI becomes more prevalent, responsible development is crucial:

- Ethical Considerations: Responsible AI seeks to ensure fairness, accountability, transparency, and safety in AI applications. This is critical as AI systems make decisions that can significantly impact individuals and communities.

- Trust Building: Companies prioritizing responsible AI practices are more likely to build trust with their customers and stakeholders, fostering a positive brand image and avoiding potential legal and reputational risks.

- Regulatory Compliance: Governments are increasingly demanding responsible AI practices. As of February 13, 2025, many companies are still struggling to implement responsible AI programs, exposing themselves to regulatory, financial, and reputational risks.

Fostering an Inclusive AI-Integrated Society

Creating an inclusive AI-integrated society is essential for equitable progress:

- Diverse Stakeholder Engagement: AI must be developed inclusively, with consultation from a diverse set of stakeholders and the broader public, to ensure technology can benefit all people and society.

- Addressing Underrepresentation: Many underrepresented groups, minorities, and people living in rural areas are often left behind due to lack of access, technological literacy, and biases inherent in AI systems6. Efforts are being made to develop AI systems that are sensitive to the needs of these groups and actively promote diversity and inclusivity.

- Critical Capabilities: Projects like the AI Capabilities Lab are working to understand the knowledge, skills, and literacies needed to achieve inclusive AI, ensuring that all members of society can benefit from AI tools and participate in their design or respond to their deployment.

By focusing on responsible development, addressing global challenges, and fostering inclusivity, we can shape a connected future where AI serves as a force for social justice, strengthening workers' rights, promoting decent work, and contributing to a more equitable society.

The Path Forward: Human-AI Collaboration

Cultivating Uniquely Human Skills in the AI Age

As AI continues to advance, certain human skills become increasingly valuable:

- Critical thinking and complex problem-solving remain essential human capabilities that complement AI's data processing abilities.
- Creativity and innovation are uniquely human traits that AI cannot fully replicate, making them crucial in the AI era.
- Emotional intelligence and empathy are vital for effective communication and leadership, areas where humans still excel over AI.
- Organizations should invest in professional development programs that focus on enhancing these cognitive skills through workshops, mentorship opportunities, and hands-on projects.

Strategies for Effective Human-AI Partnerships

To maximize the potential of human-AI collaboration:

- Identify areas where AI can add the most value by complementing human strengths and filling expertise gaps.
- Create shared spaces for AI collaboration, integrating AI tools into centralized workspaces for streamlined teamwork.
- Approach AI integration with flexibility, creativity, and curiosity rather than rigid mandates.
- Establish clear communication protocols for how AI systems explain their findings and confidence levels.
- Implement feedback loops between human team members and AI systems to fine-tune AI responses over time.

The Ongoing Need for Adaptability and Lifelong Learning

In the rapidly evolving AI landscape, continuous learning is crucial:

- Embrace lifelong learning as a critical strategy for career longevity and success in the AI era.
- Develop learning agility to quickly adapt to new technologies and changing job requirements.
- Focus on cultivating a growth mindset that embraces change and continuous improvement.
- Integrate Real-Time Learning (RTL) habits such as awareness, pattern recognition, and experimentation into professional development.

By fostering these skills and strategies, organizations and individuals can create effective human-AI partnerships that leverage the strengths of both, leading to enhanced innovation, productivity, and adaptability in the AI age.

As we draw to a close, it's evident that the future hinges not on a world dominated by artificial intelligence, but on a world enriched by it. The insights gleaned throughout this book underscore a profound opportunity: to forge a symbiotic relationship between human creativity and AI capabilities. It's a path where we leverage AI as a powerful tool to amplify our cognitive abilities, address global challenges, and create a more connected and inclusive society.

However, this path demands a conscious commitment to responsible AI development, ensuring that ethical considerations are woven into the fabric of every innovation. We must cultivate uniquely human skills, foster effective human-AI partnerships, and embrace the ongoing need for adaptability and lifelong learning.

Ultimately, the future we create will depend on our ability to navigate the complexities of this new era with wisdom, foresight, and a deep understanding of the potential that lies within the synergy of human and artificial intelligence. As we bridge these two worlds, let us strive to build a future where technology empowers humanity, strengthens our connections, and enhances our shared experience on this planet. The journey ahead is one of collaboration, innovation, and continuous learning, and it is a journey we must embark on together.

End...

And so, we reach the end of our exploration into the fascinating and ever-evolving world of AI communication. It has been a journey filled with insights, challenges, and boundless potential. From the earliest attempts at machine dialogue to the sophisticated AI assistants of today, we've witnessed a remarkable transformation in how humans and machines interact.

The future of human-AI communication is not predetermined. It is a future we are actively shaping through our choices, our innovations, and our commitment to ethical practices. As we continue to push the boundaries of what's possible, let us remember the importance of empathy, creativity, and human connection. Let us strive to create AI systems that not only enhance our capabilities but also enrich our lives and strengthen our bonds with one another.

The conversation surrounding AI communication is far from over. It is an ongoing dialogue that will require the collective wisdom of technologists, ethicists, policymakers, and individuals from all walks of life. May this book serve as a catalyst for further exploration, innovation, and responsible development in this exciting and transformative field. The future is ours to create, together.

Appendix A: Glossary of AI Communication Terms

Below is a comprehensive glossary of key terms and concepts related to AI communication, designed to help readers understand the technical language and ideas discussed throughout the book.

Term	Definition
Artificial Intelligence (AI)	The simulation of human intelligence in machines that are programmed to think, learn, and make decisions.
Natural Language Processing (NLP)	A branch of AI focused on enabling machines to understand, interpret, and respond to human language.
Generative AI	AI systems that create new content (e.g., text, images, music) based on patterns learned from training data.
Large Language Model (LLM)	A neural network trained on massive text datasets to generate human-like language outputs.
Chatbot	Software applications that simulate human conversation through text or voice interactions.
Brain-Computer Interface (BCI)	A technology that creates direct communication pathways between the brain and external devices.
Deep Learning	A subset of machine learning using neural networks with multiple layers to analyze data and make predictions.

Prompt	The input or instruction provided by a user to guide an AI system in generating a response.
Hallucination	When an AI confidently generates incorrect or nonsensical information as if it were factual.
Bias (in AI)	Systematic errors in AI models caused by flawed training data, leading to unfair or discriminatory outcomes.
Explainable AI (XAI)	AI systems designed to provide transparency by explaining how decisions are made.
Ethical AI	The practice of designing and deploying AI systems in ways that prioritize fairness, accountability, and safety.
Generative Pre-trained Transformer (GPT)	A type of LLM architecture used for tasks like text generation, translation, and summarization.
Reinforcement Learning from Human Feedback (RLHF)	A training method where human feedback is used to fine-tune an AI model's responses.
Token	The smallest unit of text processed by an LLM, such as a word fragment or punctuation mark.
Anthropomorphism	The attribution of human traits or emotions to non-human entities like AI systems or robots.
Conversational AI	AI systems designed to simulate natural conversations using NLP and generative techniques.
Generative Adversarial Network (GAN)	A type of deep learning model used to generate realistic content such as images or videos.
Autonomous Systems	Machines capable of performing tasks without direct human

	intervention, often guided by AI algorithms.

This glossary serves as a quick reference for readers navigating the technical terminology used in discussions about human-AI communication. It highlights foundational concepts while providing clarity on more complex ideas.

Appendix B: Timeline of AI Communication Milestones

1950: Alan Turing proposes the Turing Test, laying the foundation for evaluating machine intelligence.

1952: Arthur Samuel creates a self-learning checkers program, an early demonstration of machine learning.

1955: The Logic Theorist, considered the first AI program, is developed.

1956: The term 'artificial intelligence' is coined at the Dartmouth Conference, marking the formal birth of AI as a field.

1966: ELIZA, one of the world's earliest chatbots, is created at MIT, pioneering natural language processing.

2007: The first working AI programs are written to run on the Ferranti Mark 1 machine at the University of Manchester.

2020: Microsoft introduces Turing Natural Language Generation (T-NLG), the "largest language model ever published at 17 billion parameters" in February.

2020: OpenAI introduces GPT-3, a state-of-the-art autoregressive language model, in May.

2022: ChatGPT, an AI chatbot developed by OpenAI, debuts in November, built on top of the GPT-3.5 large language model.

2023: OpenAI's GPT-4 model is released in March, regarded as an impressive improvement over GPT-3.5 with multimodal capabilities.

2023: Google releases its chatbot Google Bard, based on the LaMDA and PaLM large language models, in March.

2023: Google announces Bard's transition from LaMDA to PaLM2, a more advanced language model, in May.

2023: Google releases Gemini 1.0 Ultra.

2024: Google releases Gemini 1.5 in limited beta, capable of context length up to 1 million tokens, on February.

2024: OpenAI publicly announces Sora, a text-to-video model for generating videos up to a minute long, on February

2025: Mistral AI releases Le Chat, an AI assistant able to answer up to 1,000 words per second, on February.

This timeline showcases the rapid evolution of AI communication technologies, from early chatbots to sophisticated language models capable of generating human-like text, images, and even videos.

Appendix C: Ethical Guidelines for AI Development

1. Transparency and Disclosure
    - Label AI-generated content clearly
    - Disclose how and when AI is used
    - Do not present AI agents as humans
2. Accuracy and Reliability
    - Verify AI-generated content against trusted sources
    - Implement fact-checking processes for AI outputs
    - Ensure AI systems achieve high levels of accuracy and reliability
3. Fairness and Bias Mitigation
    - Regularly check AI systems for bias
    - Use diverse and representative datasets for training
    - Implement algorithmic fairness techniques
4. Privacy and Data Protection
    - Respect users' privacy rights and follow data protection laws
    - Obtain explicit consent for using personal data in AI training

- Implement mechanisms for users to control their data

5. Accountability and Oversight

    - Establish clear lines of accountability for AI decisions
    - Maintain human oversight throughout the AI lifecycle
    - Conduct regular audits of AI systems

6. Safety and Security

    - Prioritize the safety of human life, health, and the environment
    - Protect AI systems from cyber threats and vulnerabilities
    - Implement robust security measures for AI tools and data

7. Interpretability and Documentation

    - Design AI systems to be interpretable and explainable
    - Document design decisions and development protocols
    - Provide clear explanations of AI decision-making processes

8. Continuous Learning and Improvement

    - Commit to ongoing monitoring and evaluation of AI systems
    - Adapt through feedback loops and user education
    - Stay current on AI advancements and potential risks

9. Inclusiveness and Stakeholder Engagement

- Engage diverse perspectives in AI development and deployment
- Collaborate with multiple stakeholders for inclusive AI governance
- Consider the societal impact of AI communication technologies

10. Proportionality and Necessity

    - Ensure AI use does not exceed what is necessary for legitimate aims
    - Conduct risk assessments to prevent potential harms
    - Balance transparency with other principles like privacy and security

Appendix D: AI Communication Tools and Platforms

1. ChatGPT
   A large language model that generates human-like text responses. It can be used for content creation, answering questions, and general conversation.

2. ClickUp
   A productivity platform with AI-powered features like ClickUp Brain for automating email drafts and summarizing meetings.

3. Yatter AI
   A chatbot that enhances communication on WhatsApp and Telegram, offering real-time message streaming and template creation.

4. Notta
   An AI transcription service that converts recorded speech into text, auto-joins meetings for transcription, and supports multiple languages.

5. Synthesia
   An AI-powered video generation and editing tool that can create videos from text, PowerPoint presentations, PDFs, or URLs.

6. Claude
   An AI assistant capable of engaging in conversations and performing various tasks.

7. Gemini
   Google's advanced AI model for natural language processing and generation.

8. Grammarly

   An AI-powered writing assistant that checks grammar, spelling, and style.

9. Perplexity

   An AI-powered search engine that provides more contextual and detailed answers to queries.

10. Tidio AI

    An AI-powered customer service platform that can handle customer inquiries and support tasks.

These tools represent a range of AI-powered communication technologies, from chatbots and virtual assistants to productivity enhancers and content creation aids. They demonstrate the diverse applications of AI in modern communication, offering capabilities that can streamline workflows, improve customer interactions, and enhance overall productivity.

Appendix E: Further Reading and Resources

Books:

1. "AI for Communication" by David J. Gunkel (2024)
   A comprehensive exploration of AI applications in communication, covering topics like machine translation, natural language processing, and social robotics.

2. "Research Handbook on Artificial Intelligence and Communication" edited by various scholars (2023)
   An extensive collection of research from over 50 international experts, examining the intersections between AI and communication.

Articles and Research Papers:

1. "Towards More Human-like AI Communication: A Review of Emergent Communication Research" by Nicolo' Brandizzi et al. (2023)
   An in-depth review of emergent communication research, focusing on developing AI agents capable of using natural language effectively.

2. "Artificial intelligence in communication impacts language and social relationships" in Nature Scientific Reports (2023)
   A study examining how AI-generated messages influence human communication behavior and social relationships.

Websites and Online Resources:

1. Frontiers Research Topic: "AI and Communication"
   An interdisciplinary exploration of AI's effects on society's communication, covering various aspects including science and environmental communication.

2. Taylor & Francis eBooks: AI for Communication
   Offers additional resources and materials related to AI in communication.

3. arXiv.org: Computation and Language section
   A repository of preprint research papers on AI and communication, regularly updated with new studies.

These resources provide a mix of academic research, practical insights, and theoretical frameworks for readers interested in exploring various aspects of AI in communication. They cover topics ranging from the technical aspects of AI development to the social and ethical implications of AI-human interactions.

Appendix F: Case Studies in Human-AI Collaboration

Healthcare: AI-Assisted MRI Analysis
In radiology departments, AI systems are enhancing the diagnostic capabilities of human radiologists:

- AI rapidly processes complex MRI data, highlighting potential abnormalities.
- Radiologists focus on critical aspects of diagnosis, reducing fatigue-related errors.
- This collaboration improves diagnostic accuracy and efficiency.

Lesson learned: AI augments human expertise rather than replacing it, allowing medical professionals to spend more time on patient care.

Mental Health Support: TalkLife Platform
The TalkLife platform demonstrates how AI can enhance human emotional intelligence in mental health support:

- Peer supporters working alongside AI assistance showed a 19.6% increase in conversational empathy.
- Those initially struggling with providing support demonstrated a 38.9% improvement when aided by AI suggestions.

Best practice: Use AI to augment human emotional capabilities rather than attempting to replace human interaction entirely.

Creative Industries: Sketch-RNN Project
The Sketch-RNN project showcases interactive collaboration between artists and AI:

- As humans begin drawing, the AI system suggests complementary strokes and creative directions.
- This partnership opens new possibilities for artistic exploration while maintaining human creative control.

Lesson learned: Effective human-AI collaboration in creative fields requires maintaining human agency and artistic vision.

Education: Intelligent Tutoring Systems (ITS)
Research suggests that collaborating with an ITS can be as effective for mastering skills and knowledge as working one-on-one with a human tutor:

- AI adapts to each student's needs, providing personalized learning experiences.
- Human teachers offer guidance and emotional support, complementing the AI's capabilities.
- Best practice: Combine AI's ability to personalize content with human teachers' expertise in providing holistic educational support.

Emergency Medicine: AI-Assisted Triage
In emergency departments, AI-assisted diagnostic tools are improving patient care:

- AI systems rapidly process incoming patient data, including imaging results.
- Healthcare providers apply their clinical judgment and emotional intelligence to make final decisions.

- This collaboration enables faster intervention in critical cases.

Lesson learned: Clear roles and responsibilities between AI systems and human healthcare providers are crucial for effective emergency care.

These case studies demonstrate that successful human-AI collaboration depends on leveraging the unique strengths of both human and artificial intelligence while acknowledging their respective limitations. By following these best practices and learning from these examples, organizations can create more resilient and effective teams that maximize the potential of both human and AI capabilities.

Appendix G: AI Communication Research Institutions and Organizations

1. UNSW AI Institute (University of New South Wales, Australia)

   - Supports over 300 academics and 50+ research groups across multiple faculties
   - Focus on AI development, application, and translation
   - Promotes interdisciplinary collaborations and research commercialization

2. Centre for Applied Artificial Intelligence (Macquarie University, Australia)

   - Established in 2019
   - Focuses on AI and process automation
   - Collaborates with industry partners on various AI applications

3. Centre for Artificial Intelligence Research and Optimisation (AIRO) (Torrens University, Australia)

   - Explores AI and smart technologies for future city applications
   - Focuses on service design and human-centric design
   - Addresses challenges in smart aged home care, digital twin, urban planning, and automated health services

4. AI Communications (European Association for Artificial Intelligence)

- Journal covering the whole AI community
- Focuses on scientific institutions and commercial/industrial companies

5. Universities Australia Working Group on AI in Research

   - Supports the higher education sector in adapting to AI
   - Develops resources for universities on the ethical use of AI in research

6. Swinburne University of Technology (Australia)

   - Offers courses on "Communicating with AI"
   - Explores current and emergent practices for using AI in communication

These institutions and organizations are at the forefront of AI communication technology research and development, contributing to advancements in the field through academic studies, industry collaborations, and policy recommendations.

Glossary of AI Communication Terms

Artificial Intelligence (AI): The simulation of human intelligence in machines programmed to think and learn like humans.

Automatic Speech Recognition (ASR): Technology that transcribes spoken language into text9. Also known as computer speech recognition.

Conversational AI: AI systems capable of interacting with humans in human-like conversations.

Deep Learning: A function of AI that imitates the human brain by learning from data structure. A class of neural networks with one or more layers used for image recognition and processing\.

Generative AI (GenAI): An emerging field within AI that creates new content such as text, images, voice, video, and code by learning from data patterns.

Large Language Model (LLM): A type of system that enables generative AI, designed to understand human language and generate content from that.

Machine Learning (ML): A subset of AI that allows computers to autonomously learn and improve without being explicitly programmed.

Natural Language Generation (NLG): The process by which a machine turns structured data into text or speech that humans can understand.

Natural Language Processing (NLP): A field of AI that deals with the ability of computer systems to understand and generate human language.

Natural Language Understanding (NLU): The AI's capability to comprehend and interpret human language in a meaningful way. A subfield of NLP that focuses on enabling computers to comprehend and interpret the meaning of human language by extracting meaning, context, and intent from text data.

Prompting: The art of crafting clear instructions and specific details to guide AI tools towards a desired output.

Footnote

As someone deeply involved in guiding organizations through digital transformations, I, Vishakha Marwah, Program manager, brought a unique perspective to this project. My work has highlighted the critical importance of effective communication in the age of AI. I believe this book offers valuable insights into how we can leverage AI not just as a tool, but as a partner in fostering more meaningful and productive human interactions. Being a Certified Scrum Master and Agile Coach, I was able to give firsthand experience of communication challenges.

About Author

Author Biography: Vishakha Marwah is a dynamic leader with over 18 years of experience delivering large-scale transformation programs and data-driven solutions for prominent global clients. As a Senior Manager, she specializes in leading high-impact technology initiatives, driving strategic decision-making, and managing globally-spread cross-functional teams. Her expertise in agile methodologies, data analytics, and cloud migration brings a wealth of practical knowledge to this discussion of AI communication

www.ingramcontent.com/pod-product-compliance
Lightning Source LLC
LaVergne TN
LVHW021155160826
845679LV00024B/2135

9798897440030